From Chaos to Clarity

Getting Unstuck & Creating a Life You Love

Alex Bratty

Alex Bratty Books are available for order through
Ingram Press Catalogues

Alex Bratty
Visit my websites at www.alexbratty.com
and www.alexbrattybooks.com

Printed in the United States of America
First Printing: September 2015
Published by Sojourn Publishing, LLC

ISBN: 978-1-62747-153-4
Ebook ISBN: 978-1-62747-154-1

Praise for *From Chaos to Clarity: Getting Unstuck & Creating a Life You Love*

"Alex brilliantly brings two unlikely worlds together by sharing her corporate background with her experience of transformation and spiritual growth. She takes you on a journey of self-discovery and connection to your Divine Self. I was inspired by her stories and so related to the challenges she faced. She shares invaluable information and techniques to free you from your own challenges. A must read for anyone who gets stuck in their limiting beliefs and is ready to move forward and experience more meaning and purpose in their life."

– Lisa Ulshafer,
Author of Journey with an Angel

"A powerful book that charts a clear course from the darkness of being stuck to the bright light of clarity and opportunity. Read this book and transform your life!"

– Tom Bird,
Renowned Book Whisperer
& Best-Selling Author

"A profound renewal of self! With passion and enthusiasm, Alex gives us a step-by-step guide to reprogramming our belief system. It's Your Turn to leave burnout, depression, and exhaustion behind. You only have to read this book once to reach the richness

and goodness that is within you. UNSTUCK is a personal transformation experience."

– Tom Puetz,
Author of *Secret Choices,* http://tompuetz.com

"An inspiring call to self-action and betterment, packaged in an easily digestible and approachable form. This book will help to prepare, challenge and guide the reader to receiving the amazing life that awaits those willing to receive it, by re-calibrating from an outward to an inward focus in the personal search for answers and direction."

– James "Mick" Andzulis,
MBA, MSF, PhD, Assistant Professor,
Louisiana State University

"Alex's honest portrayal of her life struggles and challenges creates such a powerful connection with the reader. It's impossible to read this book and not feel like she's walked in your shoes. And, Alex's willingness to share what she learned in the process of overcoming those obstacles – the good, the bad, and ugly – leaves the reader with a clear blueprint and the tools needed to build a better life."

– Rob Autry,
Founder of Meeting Street Research

"Stuck in your life? Through her own clear voice and life experiences, Alex delivers a practical guide on how to find the courage to become 'unstuck' and the freedom to find your life's purpose. I wish I had this

book as I coached employees on finding their true passion. It is practical, honest, and guarantees the reader can discover their own divine purpose. A definite read for you and a great gift for anyone who might be stuck!"

– Barbara Bras,
Author & Vice President for
Best Western International (retired)

"Want to identify and take charge of those seemingly mysterious forces charting your course through life? With an enticing blend of her own experience to intrigue you and practical tools to engage you, Alex Bratty delivers a book that can be personal, meaningful and useful to everyone."

– Ruth How,
PUMA Head of Marketing -
UK, Ireland, BeNeLux

"Alex Bratty shares stories of her struggle to overcome obstacles that had caused her to feel stuck in life. In this book, she helps you figure out what you really want in life, not what you are supposed to want."

– David Copeland,
Associate Professor,
University of Nevada, Las Vegas

"In this book, Alex shares and gives of her life to help others, just as I have seen her do in person with countless people over the years. Read this book, follow her guidance, and find success!"

– Jack Childs,
President of the National Wrestling
Coaches Association & Drexel University
Head Wrestling Coach (retired)

"Practical, inspired wisdom from one who has walked this road."

– Angela Ditch,
Author, Speaker & Founder of the
Body Ascension Lens

"An honest evaluation of the mind maze that keeps us stuck. Practical wisdom that untangles the thought paradigms that hold us hostage and perpetuate our present circumstances. Expose the cause culprit and a new world opens up. From Chaos to Clarity *perfectly shifts the mind set to expecting and receiving more."*

– Susan Diane Howell, MBA,
Director of the Academy of Diva Arts

Dedication

To Rich and Sunny. You will always be my pack.

Acknowledgements

I would like to express my deepest gratitude and appreciation to all the people who made this book possible.

Thanks to Tom Bird, RamaJon Cogan, Mary Stevenson, and the rest of the fantastic team at Sojourn Publishing. Without their soul-centered guidance, support, and expertise, this book would still be inside me, instead of on these pages.

Thanks to Lisa Ulshafer, who has been an inspiration and constant guiding light over the last few years. As the proverb goes, "When the student is ready, the teacher will appear." She was my teacher who appeared when I needed a teacher most: when I was ready to really face what was keeping me stuck, and ready to make the changes that would ultimately transform my life.

Thanks to Lynn Carroll and Rebecca Everett, who have also helped guide me on my journey of personal development. Each of these amazing women understood me, and encouraged me to step into my life's purpose and follow my dreams.

Thanks to Christy Whitman and her team at the Quantum Success Coaching Academy, who taught me how to become a life coach so I could fulfill my calling to help others navigate their life journeys. And thanks also to Pam Henry and Diane Linsley, both of whom were the best coaching "buddies" I could have asked for during my certification training.

Thanks to Marie Forleo and Kathy Caprino, who motivated me to build my professional life the way I really want it, rather than the way I thought it should be.

Thanks to Louise Hay, who wrote *You Can Heal Your Life*. It was the very first book I read on my transformational journey, and it opened me up to a whole new way of thinking about my life and the universe.

Thanks to Julian Krinsky, Adrian Castelli, Jack Childs, Robin Garfield, Bill McInturff, and Neil Newhouse for being incredible mentors and motivators during some of my formative professional years.

Thanks to all my family, friends, clients, and fellow authors who have all been cheerleaders as I wrote this book and made major transitions in my life over the last few years.

Finally, and most importantly, I want to thank my husband, for his unwavering love, devotion, and support. He saw who I was at my core, and knew my true self before I was able to.

Contents

Foreword
by Christy Whitman

Many a success story begins as a tale of adversity. Witnessing another triumph over difficulty ignites something deep within us, both because it speaks to the enduring strength of the human spirit, but more importantly, because it awakens us to the reality that what is possible for one is possible for all, and that we too are capable of this kind of transformation.

Although I love success stories – and as someone who's re-created virtually every area of my life many times over and coached thousands of others to do the same, I have certainly collected a few of my own. But what's vital to take away from any inspirational tale is not the particulars of what others have created, but the process they used to create it. Once you understand the formula for shifting the way you interact with the universe around you in order to deliberately cause a different result, you can apply it anywhere.

Regardless of the level of success we've attained, every human being has had the feeling that the direction our lives are moving is in direct opposition to the direction we would like them to go. If you have picked up this book, you probably already understand that once a downward spiral starts, it tends to take on a life of its own. The more we dwell on what's not working, the worse we feel, and every annoyance, heartbreak or injustice seems to build towards the next.

This is the state of consciousness that author Alex Bratty defines as being "stuck." Anyplace in our lives where we are experiencing a lack of freedom is an indication that we are operating within this limited level of consciousness. Our perception is that other people or circumstances have the power to make us happy – or to steal that happiness from us. Not a happy place to be.

This book recounts Alex's deeply personal, true-to-life experience of the years she struggled with being stuck, and the journey she took to set herself free. And like the proverbial journey of 10,000 miles, the most pivotal moment is when we take that first step.

From Chaos to Clarity is a step-by-step, soup-to-nuts guide to reclaiming freedom, joy, love and abundance in any area of your life where you are not creating the results you desire. In it, Alex shares the insights that illumined her path of self-discovery, and offers tools and practices that you can immediately apply to re-create any aspect of your life.

Just what does it take to shift the momentum when we are genuinely frustrated, discouraged, or anxious in some important aspect of our lives? In situations or relationships that we feel powerless to change, what are those first essential steps to taking back our power? And once we've made some initial progress, how can we keep that energy alive and moving forward? These are some of the questions this book addresses head-on. Learn the art of getting unstuck, and you will forever have a reliable formula for transforming any challenge and manifesting any outcome you want to create.

Christy Whitman, NY Times Best-Selling Author
www.ChristyWhitman.com
Montreal, Canada
Summer, 2015

"Out of clutter, find simplicity.
From discord, find harmony.
In the middle of difficulty lies opportunity."
— Albert Einstein

Chapter 1
Are You Stuck?

A re you stuck? Stuck in life? Stuck in your career? Stuck in love? Stuck in relationships? Do you have feelings of disappointment, regret, or sadness, knowing that there must be more to life than what you are experiencing right now?

Do you feel frustrated – as though you are spinning your wheels and doing the same things over and over because you don't know how to get unstuck? Or, maybe you're worried about what will happen if you *do* get unstuck? Where will it go, or what will it lead to? How will your life change?

Are you anxious? Do you have feelings of tightness in your body, or a constant awareness that there is something bigger out there waiting for you – but you just don't know how to reach it?

If you have any of these feelings, then I'd like to introduce myself – because I have had *all* of these feelings, and others like them, for most of my life. And, I'm here to tell you that if I can get unstuck – then so can you.

It has taken me a long time to get here. I came to this place through a journey that was full of twists and turns. Some of it definitely wasn't pretty, but it has all led me to this place where I am today. In writing to you, I'm sharing my experience about what I have learned, and how I am using it to find more fulfillment, to gain clarity about who I am and my purpose in life.

If you picked up this book, it means you are stuck or blocked or frustrated by how some things are going in your life. My hope is that you will find my story helpful, that you may see some of yourself in it, and that by using the tools I provide, you can also find the clarity, happiness, and ease you are seeking in your life.

During much of my life, I often found myself in a state of just knowing that there was something greater than me, and something greater that I was to be doing – but having no sense of exactly what that was.

Without any understanding or direction of that greater meaning, I just plowed ahead, following the path I thought I *should* be on, hoping that one day I'd wake up with the clarity and creativity I so desired. I used to read all manner of materials – newspapers, books, magazines – in the hope that the wide range of content would spark an idea or create the flash of insight I was looking for.

I used to think: if only I could have a really cool idea, I'd be set. I used to yearn for this inspiration. I sensed that there was so much more I was to understand or to see in life, but I just couldn't reach it. It was as though there were a fog or a veil between me and what I was to know, or to be, or to do. It felt close, but out of reach at the same time. It was so frustrating. I just couldn't seem to connect to what I needed to know, and I felt lost without this missing vision and comprehension.

I used to engage in all kinds of work and activities that distracted me from this yearning, and I felt a deep sense of aloneness that I was the only person going through all of this. I know now that I wasn't alone in feeling lost, stuck, and frustrated – many of us experience these emotions.

Now, working as a life coach, I see this all the time. We are uncertain in ourselves, in our purpose, in our abilities and skills. It saddens me that so many of us spend our days thinking these thoughts, and running what I call the "negative programs" in our minds.

Do you ever find yourself engaged in negative chatter in your head? You might have a good idea, but you immediately put yourself down and say, "That's crazy," or "How could I possibly do that?" Or, perhaps that voice tells you that someone – a parent, a spouse, a partner, a sibling, a friend – won't approve? We all have thoughts like these from time to time, and we often believe them. When that happens, we keep ourselves stuck, running in place, playing small and safe. That's okay. There's usually a reason you have these thoughts or feelings – and we're going to uncover all of that in this book.

But first, let's be clear: wherever you are in your life journey is okay. It's where you are meant to be right now. For without all the experiences that led you to this point, and without all the experiences that you are having right now in the present, you wouldn't be who you are today. None of it is wrong. In fact, all of it is right, because it has brought you to this place, ready to read this book – and get unstuck.

You see, just because we are in a particular place doesn't mean it has to stay that way, and that we have to continue along our same path. I'm here to tell you that we all have the power and strength inside us to become the people we really want to be, to live the lives we really want to have, and to allow love, joy, openness, creativity, and abundance to flow freely into our lives.

You might be reading this and thinking, "Okay, but what's the catch?" Or, your negative programming and chatter might be kicking in right around now, saying, "Yeah, right, like I can have what I want!"

If you're hearing the negative voices, ask them to stop, just for a few minutes, while you read on and digest more of what I have to say. Just put the voices off to the side for now. We'll come back to them later, but for now, all they need to do is be quiet and let you connect with what I'm saying.

Maybe you've tried to run from or avoid that feeling of being stuck. You may have turned to drugs or alcohol, or you may find yourself in destructive relationships. Or, maybe you have already tried lots of different things to try to get unstuck: workshops, courses, self-help books, energy healing, massage, acupuncture, therapy, coaching, counseling, meditation – and the list could go on and on. Perhaps you haven't done anything yet. Wherever you are with your feeling of "stuckness" is just fine.

You are not alone, and I have been where you are: searching for answers; looking for the truth. I'll give you the punchline right now, so that it won't be buried deep in this book. Guess what? The answer is simple – it's all inside you.

That's right. Every single thing you are yearning for, every dream, every desire, every piece of guidance. It's all inside you. You actually have all the answers you'll ever need. And, you have always had them.

That's why, for so long, I felt that what I wanted to understand or know was so close. It was inside of me, and it couldn't be any closer than that! Yet, at the same time, it felt out of reach because I didn't know how to access it. Not only that, I didn't know what was in there, and what it would mean to unlock it all.

This book gives you a roadmap for how to reach all the richness and goodness that is within you. It is going to help you identify the reasons you have been feeling stuck, or frustrated, or anxious. It is designed to help you get unstuck, to be the person you want to be, to live the life you want. It gives you the tools you need, to deal with and move past whatever is blocking you and keeping you stuck. As you do that, you begin the journey to find your true meaning, your true self, and your true joy and freedom in life. It will teach you how to tap into the real you, so that you can open yourself up, reconnect with your inner guidance, and get answers to your questions.

Here's the best part. You only have to read this book once to get your own personal roadmap for the life you want to create. Once you have read it, it is a resource for life. It's a lifetime guide – a GPS for your heart and soul – that can always help you find your way, even in the darkest hour or the murkiest situation. Use the processes I provide, and you will find your way to the light, to freedom, and to personal growth.

I discovered these tools and resources as I worked through getting unstuck in my own life. I had a fifteen-year career conducting public-opinion and market research for major corporations and professional organizations. I worked my way up the ranks, and became a partner in a prominent research firm, based in Washington, D.C. From the outside, it looked as if I had it all. I was highly prosperous, and my clients loved me. I was often on the road for them, conducting focus groups, presenting findings, attending strategy meetings. It was a lucrative and successful career, yet I wasn't fulfilled and happy. I was grinding through my days like nails on a chalkboard – something didn't feel right, something didn't fit. But, I didn't know what it was. I was stuck.

I also had periods in my personal life where I felt stuck or trapped. I found myself living the life I thought I *should*, rather than the one I wanted. I dated on and off in my early twenties, never finding anyone who held my interest. I was always looking for the next person or the next distraction. I married my first husband after a year and half of dating, because it was the logical next step. Just four years later, we were divorced. It was an amicable separation, in large part because we had different expectations of the marriage, and we'd lost our sense of shared purpose.

I was always moving through life looking for someone or something to be the solution, to bring me happiness, to answer my questions – or to help me get unstuck. I also thought that fixing one part of my life would help fix everything else. For me, the part that always felt the most stuck and that took up most of my energy and attention was my professional life – that if I could just get unstuck in how I felt about my career, the rest of my life would be fine.

But, it's more than that – it's always more than that. Indeed, for those of you who think it's just one area of your life that needs to be fixed or unstuck, I have some news: it's probably not. More likely, it's bigger than just one issue or one area. Trust me, I know. I know from my own personal-transformation experience, and I know from my work as a life coach.

Some of you may be vigorously protesting that point right now, saying, "Not me. I know it's just my career, or just my marriage, or just my living accommodations, or just my financial situation." But, is that really the case? Usually it's not, but we fool ourselves into thinking it is – and it contributes to our being stuck. This happened to me. I was singularly focused that my career was the source of my being stuck. I soon discovered that it was much more than that. Only when I began to look at the bigger picture of my life did things start to get unstuck, and move forward again.

I don't say this to overwhelm you, but rather to bring your attention to what you – like me – may have fallen asleep to. Over multiple years of being stuck, I convinced myself of so many things. I convinced myself that this was the life I was living, so I *should* get on board with what it entailed. I convinced myself that I belonged in a rigorous professional culture where feeling and emotions took a back seat in the workplace. I convinced myself that because I was good at what I was doing, and making the money I'd always dreamed of, that I *should* like it and stay in it.

Where did these messages come from? Why did I convince myself of all this? So many of us convince ourselves of things that are not our own truths. When this happens, it's because we're operating from the deeply held or negative programs of belief in our minds, and listening to the negative chatter playing over and over.

Beneath all these things I had convinced myself of were long-held beliefs and programs that I wasn't good enough; that I wasn't smart enough; that I didn't deserve the wealth and success of my career; that I wasn't deserving of love or a family; that I wasn't capable of having a family and having a career; that I wasn't able to be happy in a career *and* in my personal life.

At the time, these didn't seem like choices I had made. I felt as though I had to follow the roads I went down. But, they were all choices: all decisions that I made at various points along the way that contributed to my journey – and to this perpetual feeling deep down that I was stuck, and that if only I could move beyond this stuckness, something better lay ahead.

How many decisions and choices have you made that contributed to your being stuck? It may be many or may it be few. It doesn't matter. You made them, and this is where you are. Your situation right now is what it is, and you are right where you need to be. It's your unique journey. Don't make it wrong, and don't make yourself wrong. Accept it for what it is.

The key point is that it doesn't have to stay this way. You can't change the past. But you can change how you approach things in the present, and set yourself up for a more fulfilling life where you are better able to make decisions and choices that serve you well in the future.

It's Your Turn:

Start now by taking a few moments to identify the areas that cause you the most pain or frustration. It is the first step on your journey of healing them, and moving to a better place.

⌘ Get quiet; sit up straight with your feet on the floor and your arms and legs uncrossed. Close your eyes and take a deep breath in through your nose, and exhale strongly out through your mouth. Repeat this four more times. Really take the time with this breathing to calm and center yourself.

⌘ Ask yourself these questions, and listen for the answers:
  – In what areas of my life do I feel stuck or anxious or frustrated?
  – Is it just these specific areas where I have issues to address, or is this where the frustration or anxiety primarily shows up?
  – Do I have patterns of behavior that run through various aspects of my life?

Write down the answers as they come to you. Are you surprised by them? Or are these answers what you expected?

_____

_____

_____

_____

_____

Chapter 2
Look Inside For Answers

So many of us look outside of ourselves to find the answers to our problems or the way to get unstuck. I know I did for many years – on both a personal and a professional level. I was looking for a partner in life to fill the emptiness I felt in my heart. I used my professional life for validation about my worth and value in the world. It took me a long time to figure out that looking to other people, situations, or achievements was not the solution.

For years, I felt so alone and lost. I attributed this to not having a significant other. I thought I wasn't meeting the right guy, but after years of dating, I began to understand a different truth. It was not about them; it was about me. I was disconnected from myself, and it meant I was unable to connect on a truly intimate level with someone else. That was the reason I wasn't finding happiness in relationships. As long as I kept looking to others to fill the void, I would continue feeling this way.

We have to be whole, complete, and happy within ourselves – first. This is not ground-breaking information, but so many of us still don't get it. I didn't get it for the longest time. I found myself in a marriage where we just couldn't communicate. He couldn't hear my needs, and I couldn't hear his. It ultimately ended in divorce after multiple efforts at therapy. Even when we had bared our vulnerable souls in counseling, we still weren't in a place to be what we needed for each other. I couldn't be the wife he wanted, and he couldn't be the husband I wanted. It was an odd union of "opposites attract." My family had all politely commented on how different he and I were, and I knew the underlying implication was that they didn't think it would work.

They were right. It didn't. I hadn't listened to my intuition, which was desperately telling me that even though I loved and cherished so many things about him, they would not make up for the other parts that were missing for me. I understand now that this first marriage didn't work because I didn't know myself well enough, and I was looking for him to fix whatever I felt was missing or wrong with me.

Of course, he couldn't do that. No other person can. The reasons I thought I had married were not the same as how I saw them once we were divorced, when there was distance between us and the experience. I had married because I thought I *should*. I had found a wonderful guy, we loved each other, and we had been dating for over a year. We were in our late twenties; everyone around us seemed to be getting married; I guess we *should*, too. Hmmm, any time you find yourself saying "I should," stop and question it immediately – but we'll get to that later.

I spent much of my twenties wondering what I wanted in relationships. I had all kinds of preconceived notions of what a relationship *should* look like. Some of this came from my childhood, where I had witnessed several very unhappy marriages in my family.

When I was a child visiting my friends' homes, where their parents were still together, I had trouble understanding the dynamic. It felt too calm, too happy. I was sure it was too good to be true. As a teenager, I was allowed to go on vacation with a friend and her family. I was with them in a small camper for a week, and traveling together in the car. I didn't see fighting. Yes, I saw disagreements and a few squabbles between siblings, but her mom and dad were warm and loving to one another, they had fun with each other, and they didn't fight.

This was an eye-opener for me. My whole life, I had witnessed doors slamming and people storming out on one another; sometimes physical abuse, and certainly verbal and mental abuse. I thought that this was normal, because I didn't know any other way of being. I also grew up thinking divorce was pretty standard, and that parents who stayed together were unusual, not the norm.

I'm not assigning blame to anyone, just stating the facts that this was my concept of marriage and family life. With these perceptions, it actually astounds me that I was able to marry at all, that first time around. I had often had stormy relationships prior to that. There would be drama, fights, making up. If there wasn't drama, I felt bored. Then along came my first husband-to-be. He was so calm and centered. I felt safe and secure for the first time ever in a relationship, and I thought he could give me that stabilizing force I so desperately needed in my life.

He did, for a while. But, because I didn't recognize that I had to stabilize myself and reprogram most of my underlying beliefs about relationships and marriage, it's hardly surprising that it all ended the way it did. I think we both learned a lot from our time together, and we parted as friends. We still check in from time to time on birthdays or holidays, in fact, and I will always love him for the delightful person he is, and for all our shared experiences.

After I realized I was yet another divorce statistic, I knew I had to start going inwards for answers. I started seeing a therapist once a week because I thought my friends would start to disown me. I was doing so much analysis and searching for answers that they were all tired of hearing about it. So, I decided to pay someone to listen to me. It proved to be a much more valuable experience than just a hired ear.

This wasn't my first encounter with therapy. My husband and I had gone for a year to couples counseling. That was helpful, but it didn't allow for me to truly start answering some questions for myself, and figuring out more about what I wanted in my personal life. When I started therapy for myself and for what I was going through, I was so ashamed to be getting a divorce – so ashamed to have failed in such a big and public way.

Yet, once again, much of that was outer-facing. I was worried what other people would think, not what *I* was thinking or feeling. As I worked through this shame, it became apparent that I was ashamed of myself – for an unsuccessful marriage, and for having gotten married in the first place. Deep down I knew it might not work, yet I did it anyway. No doubt, having that subconscious thought doomed it from the start, because I ultimately didn't believe in myself or in us as a couple. I was more in love with the *idea* of us, and of being married, than the reality of it.

As I examined this further and looked deeper into my soul, I realized that I was trying to find a partner who would heal all my wounds from childhood and make it all better. That sounds ridiculous when said out loud or written here, but so many of us search for that one person who can fix it all.

I realized I had to confront many insecurities and issues that I'd been carrying with me for years. I have since remarried, and I now enjoy a healthy, loving, and nurturing relationship with my husband. But, if I hadn't done my inner work to be more secure and happy within myself, I know that wouldn't be the case. I would still be looking to him for all the answers to my problems.

It was the same way during my fifteen-year career in research. Everything was focused on others: was my boss happy with my work? Was I getting compliments on a job well done? I would use my accomplishments as a measure of my self-worth. Once I became a partner in my firm, it was all about getting validation from my clients and my sales. When we're in business, of course we want our clients to be happy and we want to make money. But, I was using these measures as a barometer of how valuable or worthy I was as a human being. I was looking outside of myself again for the validation I felt I needed.

I would also look outside of myself in identifying problems or trying to find solutions. I used to get so frustrated by client expectations of my time, my deliverables, how available I was to them. It felt as though I would give a hundred and ten percent, and yet they still seemed to want more. When I really looked at this situation, I realized that this made me feel disrespected. It angered me and made me ready to scream.

Upon further reflection, I understood the reality: I wasn't treating myself with respect, with compassion. I had unrealistic expectations of myself. I had decided I could do anything, get it all done in the shortest time frame, make it look great, and present it all perfectly. I was the one who agreed to the ridiculous timelines, and then reaped the pain of what I had sown. I was the one who made myself available at all times of the day and evening to respond to emails and be on conference calls. What it really came down to was that I wasn't treating myself with the respect, compassion, and love that I deserved and needed. I wasn't setting the boundaries of my availability. So, if I didn't do that, why would I expect that others would?

You see, so much of what we experience on the outside is because we're experiencing it on the inside. If we're experiencing people in our lives who don't respect us, it's very often because we're not respecting ourselves. If people show up as angry or frustrated, we might look inwards to see if we are angry or frustrated with ourselves.

This can be a hard pill to swallow. When I was first learning this concept that whatever we experience on the outside is often happening on the inside, my reaction was one of disgust and protest. "What do you mean I'm doing it to myself? They're doing it to me! They're the problem, not me! Are you saying I'm to blame? That I'm the problem?"

Well, I put that question in rather blunt terms, but the answer is, essentially, "yes." However, "blame" and "problem" are not words that I'm going to use because none of this is about blame. So, if it's not other people or situations that are the cause of our unhappiness or our stuckness, what is it? How can it be us? We only want to be happy and to have the lives we want, right? Well, yes and no…

We *think* we want the lives we desire, and that we're doing what's needed to have them. But, what usually happens is that we are not operating from a place where we give ourselves permission to be who we want to be, with the self-belief and the compassion, and the strength to move forward. Instead, we're often operating from a place of long-standing, deeply held beliefs and thoughts where we put ourselves down: keeping ourselves hidden, small and stuck in what we think we *should* be doing.

Once I recognized that I wasn't treating myself with compassion, respect, and love, it seemed like an easy fix, right? Just start doing that. But, that's where these deep-rooted beliefs come into play. I wasn't giving myself that love and respect, because subconsciously I didn't believe I deserved it. If I didn't think I truly deserved this, how could I give myself the love and compassion I needed to bring about change? And, if I didn't treat myself with love and compassion, how could I expect others to do the same?

How we treat and talk to ourselves has an impact in all areas of our lives. We may think we're just stuck in one aspect of our lives – our career, our relationships, our financial situation. But, as I mentioned earlier, it's bigger than that – it's about our whole selves. It's about what's going on inside us – our underlying beliefs and programming, and whether we are listening to the negative or the positive voices in our minds.

It's often the case that we are not very kind to ourselves. Just think about those negative voices, the tracks you keep playing in your mind. Think about how you talk to yourself. Do you ever tell yourself, "This isn't good enough," "It's not fast enough," "You need to do better," or some variation of that critical chatter?

Is there anyone in your life that you would talk to in that way? Anyone at all that you care about – whether it's a parent, a child, a sibling, a spouse, a partner, a best friend, a roommate – would you say these things to them? I'm pretty sure your answer is, "No." Okay, so then why do we say them to ourselves? If we keep running these negative tracks, we keep ourselves stuck in place.

If we can identify that we need to start with ourselves and not others, why do we stay stuck? Many of us feel this stuckness, but few of us do anything about it – why is that? Well, believe it or not, this happens because it's actually easier to stay stuck than to unstick ourselves.

Some of us have been stuck for so long that doing anything else would mean change. And, we all know what change means: the dreaded unknown. It's scary, and we have no idea what might happen if we change. Worse yet, we're talking about making changes to ourselves, to our inner beings. For most of us, this is scarier than anything else, for it requires going deep into ourselves to understand what lies below the surface.

So we resist the change, and all the while we keep ourselves more stuck than before. For the only way to get unstuck is to make some changes within. If we're not ready to make change, then we're not ready to connect with ourselves, and we're not ready to get unstuck.

I'm not going to sugarcoat this – it can be a challenging ride to make these inner changes. But what about the reward? Oh, the reward is so fulfilling, so full of joy, and so expansive! Is it going to be a little scary or difficult at times? Yes. But what's on the other side is so worth the effort, you'll wonder why you didn't embark on your personal-discovery journey before now.

It's Your Turn:

Think for a moment about situations or relationships you have in your life, where something or someone bothers or irritates you.

⌘ Get quiet; sit up straight with your feet on the floor and your arms and legs uncrossed.

Close your eyes, and take five deep breaths to center yourself. Inhale through your nose and exhale through your mouth. As before, really take your time with this breathing to calm and center yourself.

⌘ Ask yourself some questions about the situation or relationship that bothers you:
  – What's the reason I feel bothered or irritated?
  – Why do I feel sad or angry or frustrated by the situation, or by the way someone is treating me? It might be because you feel disrespected, or it could be because you don't feel loved, or some other reason – but what is it that makes you feel that way about the situation?

_____

_____

_____

_____

_____

Now, think for a moment about how you treat yourself.

⌘ Do you treat yourself with respect, with love, with compassion?

Very often we don't. I know I didn't, and sometimes I still catch myself doing it.

_____

_____

_____

_____

_____

Now, take a moment to imagine yourself in your absolute dream life. Current limitations, such as money and time, are no object.

⌘ Just imagine what life would be like if you were unstuck, and you could be or do whatever you wanted. As you imagine this dream life, feel it in your heart and your body.

⌘ What emotions come up for you?

_____

_____

_____

_____

_____

Are you happy and joyful in this dream life? Do you wish you could have the same feelings in your life right now? You can. The way to get there, and the answers to your questions, are already within you.

So, let's get to what this stuckness and resistance are all about. Let's work on reconnecting to our true selves, looking within to see what's going on and what we need to change, so we can move to a place where that dream life you just imagined can become your reality.

Chapter 3

What Keeps Us Stuck?

Sometimes, different things keep us stuck in different ways, but one thing is always at the root of our stuck feeling or issue: our set of underlying beliefs and thoughts about ourselves and our situation.

We all have these underlying beliefs. Uncovering them is a vital step on our journey to getting unstuck. We're all running on some programming that essentially determines who we are, what we do, and where we go in life.

We're going to look at many of the thoughts and feelings that until now have been buried within us. Sometimes we may know they're there, but most of the time we're not aware of them at all because they are deep in our subconscious mind. Yet, these underlying beliefs are the programs or operating systems that we're all running on.

Think about a computer and how we use it. We only see the beautiful interface of the screen, and we use the programs and applications that have been designed for us. Underneath all that, deep in the bowels of the computer system, is the program and operating code that all of these things run on. We rarely, if ever, see this code; and unless we know computer programming, we don't understand it. It's a mystery to most of us. While we may know it's there, we largely disregard it and just operate on the surface, using the programs we need.

Our beliefs are the same way. They are deep inside us. We may not understand them yet, or even know where they came from, but they are there. Our beliefs make up our subconscious operating system. And, a belief is simply a thought that we think over and over again until it becomes a program that runs endlessly, on automatic pilot, in our subconscious mind.

This programming of beliefs and these repetitive thoughts are the source of what keeps us stuck. Even when we say we want to do or be something different, if our subconscious mind is programmed to be thinking the opposite, it essentially undermines what we're trying to do – and it keeps us stuck.

Subconsciously, if we feel that we don't really want something, or we can't do it, or we don't deserve it, then guess what? It won't happen. We will not create or manifest it, because while we may outwardly think we want something, our subconscious mind is running on a different program and doesn't allow it to happen.

Here's where the inner work and change come in – in reprogramming our thoughts. Just as it would be a challenge to reprogram a computer, so it is challenging to reprogram our own thoughts. In fact, it's more difficult, because the human mind is so much more complex than an inanimate computer. And, for many of us, our beliefs were programmed in at an early age, so we've already been running on them for years.

I don't want to discourage you by saying that this is difficult, but I'm always going to be completely honest with you. What I'm providing in this book is the raw, unvarnished truth about what it takes to change your life and get unstuck. The inherent challenge lies in the process. It is only by embracing and working through the difficulty that you can create the inner change.

As we discussed earlier, virtually all of us resist change in our lives. We don't like it when we have to buy a different brand at the store because our favorite is out of stock. We certainly don't like it when our routines are changed. If something ends or begins in our life, it can cause real turmoil, because we are inherently resistant to change.

And yet here we are, looking at the biggest change of all: ourselves. Changing ourselves, and how we think and perceive life, is perhaps the most daunting task we can undertake. It goes right to our deepest fears. It immediately strikes a defensive chord, and we may want to keep humming an old tune, instead of composing and singing along to a new one.

But, making changes in your life, and moving towards what you truly want, will be the most rewarding and liberating thing you can ever do for yourself. You can have the life you want – you can be the person you want to be – you can do the things you want to do. But you have to be committed to challenging yourself, going deep, facing the hidden beliefs, uncovering the subconscious programming – and stepping into your own truth.

It's not easy, and it doesn't happen overnight, but I can assure you that if you commit to this work, you will be more fulfilled than you ever thought possible.

It's Your Turn:

Before we move on, take a moment to make a contract with yourself. Decide here and now that you are ready to put *you* front and center: that working on yourself – and making changes in your life – are your top priority.

This doesn't mean you have to spend hours each day doing this, but it does mean you need to set aside about fifteen minutes daily for quiet, reflective time. After reading this book, maybe you'll spend that time journaling, or maybe you'll meditate, or maybe you'll just reflect on the events of the day and what they mean. However you decide to spend this time is up to you. The important point is that you commit to devoting just a little time each day to the project of *you*.

We all spend lots of time on other projects, on watching TV, or browsing the Internet and checking out our social media. Think about where you can take back fifteen minutes each day, and devote it only to the topic of *you*. Commit to that, and schedule it just as you would schedule a conference call at work or an appointment with the doctor. Block out the time on your calendar, and follow through with it each day, just as you would with your other appointments. After all, what is more important than your own life and making it what you want it to be? Putting yourself first is not selfish, it's necessary. We cannot be of service or help to anyone else until we have first taken care of our own needs. And no one else can make these changes for you – only you can.

Now, write the contract with yourself that you are committing to at least fifteen minutes a day of focusing on you and your personal development. Sign it, date it and put a copy of it in a place where you will see it every day.

Contract with Myself
I, _____, make a commitment to myself to _____

_____

___ _____

_____

_____

Go to your calendar or your scheduler, and block out those fifteen minutes. If you can do it at the same time every day, that's even better, because you will develop it into a habit, just like brushing your teeth or washing your face every morning and night.

Okay, now that you've made a contract with yourself and committed the time each day to work on you, let's move on and identify what we hold inside us as deeply held beliefs.

First, I'll share some of mine with you, and then you can start working on your own.

For the longest time, my big ones were, "I'm not good enough," and "I'm not smart enough."

I still believed this despite a highly successful career. I had made partner in my firm faster than anyone else, I had record sales each year, and I had several repeat clients who loved my work. Yet I would constantly doubt myself, my abilities, and my skills. I didn't think I had what it took to get to where I was. There were times when I felt like a fraud, because I couldn't quite believe I'd been able to accomplish it all. Yet I had done so, and everyone around me believed in me and saw my success and my intelligence. They all thought I was smart enough and good enough.

If *they* all thought that, why didn't *I?* It's because my inner programming, and how I perceived myself, differed greatly from what they saw. My (now) husband used to say to me all the time, "Don't you get it yet? When are you going see that you *are* good enough?" And, as I used to say to him, "I guess it's like skinny jeans, honey. Even if you and everyone else say I look fabulous, I'm not wearing them unless *I believe* I look good in them."

This is true of everything in our lives. Unless we believe it at *both* the conscious and subconscious levels, we simply don't believe it. We can't believe it because our minds are running on different programs, and whatever is happening at the subconscious level can override the conscious level.

It's Your Turn:

Now, it's your turn to think about the underlying beliefs or thoughts that might be running in your subconscious mind.

⌘ Get quiet; sit up straight with your feet on the floor and your arms and legs uncrossed. Close your eyes and take those five slow and deep breaths to center yourself. Inhale through your nose and exhale through your mouth.

⌘ Think of a pattern of behavior you engage in, or a situation that bothers you – something specific in your life that you want to change. Just identify one single problem or situation for now.

⌘ Write down what it is that's bothering you, and what you want to change or see differently.

_____

_____

_____

_____

_____

⌘ Now, contemplate *why* you feel that way about it. Can you get clear on the reason something is bothering you? Really *feel* this – don't just think it.

⌘ Describe the emotions you have about this issue. Describe how you feel when it happens. Describe how you feel after it happens.

⌘ What is coming up for you? It might be that you are annoyed, or frustrated, or angry, or sad, at what is happening in this situation.

_____

_____

_____

_____

_____

Then ask yourself these questions, and listen to the answers to each:

⌘ What is my perception about this problem or situation?

⌘ Is my perception of this situation part of a broader belief or thought that I have?

⌘ Where did that belief or perception come from?

⌘ Is it really my belief, or is it someone else's belief that I am carrying with me?

⌘ Does this belief still serve my higher good; is it still providing a benefit for me?

⌘ Is this belief a block, or a bridge, to increased happiness and fulfillment?

_____

_____

_____

_____

_____

If the answer to those last few questions is that it isn't really your belief, that it isn't serving you well anymore, and that it's a block to increased happiness, then it may be time to change the belief and begin the reprogramming process.

Chapter 4

Where Do the Deeply Held Beliefs Come From?

Where do these deeply held beliefs that are programmed into our subconscious come from? Many of them have been in there for years, and so, when we ask the questions, "Where did this belief come from?" and "Is it really my belief or someone else's?" we often have to look backwards to get clarity before moving forward with reprogramming.

Looking into the past has value. It allows us to identify patterns of behavior, decisions we've made, and the directions they led us. It helps us to look at where our underlying beliefs came from. But, that doesn't mean we stay in the past. No. We look at the past to get informed, to learn from our experiences, and to help us move forward. We take what we have learned and we either choose now in the present to do things differently – or we assess that the past was just fine, and we continue doing what we've always done.

Examining these deeply held beliefs that have been programmed into our subconscious is crucial in the life-coaching work that I do. To address any issue, we first have to identify where it is rooted: what is the driving force behind the feeling, situation, or pattern of behavior? Without that root cause, we're just putting a Band-Aid over a wound that needs more thorough healing and reconnecting.

Many of us will look at deeply held beliefs, and realize that the answer to where they came from is in our childhood. This happens to all of us: what we observe and hear as children, we absorb like sponges. We've all watched how children just soak up everything around them. They're meant to – that's how we all learn and grow at an early age. But, it also means that whatever's going on in our environment around us, whatever we're hearing and seeing, becomes part of our program. Unless we are aware of it and consciously change it at some later point, it will be our program for the rest of our lives.

These deeply held beliefs may be rooted in something we saw or heard from our parents, siblings, teachers, or some other figure of authority in our life. The most common source is usually our parents, so let's just take a look at that example for a moment.

Everyone loves to point their finger at their parents. To some extent, this is valid. We are programmed as children to believe many of the things our parents said and did. If our parents were always complaining about a lack of money, or that they couldn't afford new things, we may still carry with us feelings of lack or insecurity around money. Or, as in my case, if our parents were always fighting or unloving toward one another, we may carry with us that perception of marriage and family life. If our parents told us we were stupid or not able to do something, we may still be carrying these beliefs around with us in adulthood.

As young children, the things we learn and observe from our parents get imprinted in our subconscious minds. Until we assess these beliefs and ask whether they still serve us, we just go on operating from that point of view, with that inner programming.

However, let me be clear about something here. I'm not saying we should blame our parents. Quite the opposite: I'm saying that we need to understand and forgive them. Our parents did the best they could with what they had. Forgiveness is the pathway to releasing any resentment, blame or resistance we may be feeling about what our parents said or did to us as children.

If you are finding this difficult, just think for a moment about your parents' childhoods, and what they may have grown up with; think about the type of inner programming they may have had imprinted in *their* subconscious. When they raised you, they were probably still operating from this place, and they did the best they could with their own deeply held beliefs and inner programming.

For those of you just starting out on your personal-development journey, here's something else you should know about your parents. Warning: this may blow your mind – I know it did mine, when I first learned about this concept. You chose your parents. Yes. You chose the parents you have. You see, we all choose the lessons we are to be learning in this lifetime, and in doing so, we select the parents who enable us to learn those lessons.

This may seem like a strange concept, particularly if you were adopted, or raised in foster care, or if you never knew your parents. It may be challenging to accept, since you were the child and you didn't have control over how your parents or guardians raised you, or the beliefs they instilled in you. But, by changing how you view this situation, by working from the belief that you chose your own parents and that your childhood experiences were in fact a self-selected course, you can claim ownership of your whole life. And, that puts you squarely in control of being able to change it.

The next time you want to blame your parents for something – whether it's how you feel, or what you believe – stop and remember that you chose them in order to learn something. Instead of pointing your finger, ask what it is that you were to learn. Think about that. Sit with it. Feel it. It may be uncomfortable at first, but just sit with it and understand what it is you were to be learning. Have you learned it yet? Or are you still learning the lesson, from them or in other ways?

Here's the key to unlock this stuck behavior when we want to blame our parents: they brought you up in a certain way, and you learned many things from them that have become your beliefs and your inner programming. But that doesn't mean you have to live your life by their beliefs anymore. After all, you're an adult. It's your life – when are you going to allow yourself to live your life the way *you* want?

It's Your Turn:

Take a moment and think about some of the beliefs or programs you may have picked up as a child.

⌘ Think about what your parents said, or how they behaved, on the topics of love, money, work, relationships, spirituality or religion, health, community.

⌘ Do you still carry some of those beliefs with you?

⌘ Are they serving you well, or are they limiting you and holding you back?

⌘ Is it time to change some of those beliefs?

⌘ What might be some new beliefs that would better serve you now and for the future? Can you start to make a list of new principles and beliefs to guide your life?

_____

_____

_____

_____

_____

Chapter 5

Are We Connecting with
Our Ego or Our Divine Self?

D o you often think or say, "I should…" or "I'm supposed to be…"? We all do this. We say we *should* feel a certain way or we *should* be doing this or that. Or, we're *supposed* to be going here but instead we're off somewhere else. In doing this, we're essentially making ourselves wrong.

The next time you catch yourself thinking or speaking in "should" or "supposed to be" terms, ask yourself if that's really the truth. Is it what you really want? Who does that "should" belong to? Is it in alignment with who you are, and what you want?

It's Your Turn:

⌘ Take a moment, and think of something or someone you would truly like to have in your life. I don't mean what you think you *should* want. What is it that *you truly want* in this aspect of your life?

⌘ Can you imagine yourself having what you desire, or are you experiencing feelings of resistance?

_____

_____

_____

Do you hear negative voices in your head immediately jumping in and saying things like, "You can't have that," or "You don't deserve it," "You *shouldn't* be thinking about that, you *should* be doing this instead," or, one of my favorites, "Who do you think you are to want all that?"

If you hear negative voices like these, you are not alone. In fact, virtually all of us hear these nagging doubts, and we often listen to them and put ourselves down. But, where do these negative voices come from, and are they real? Why do we believe them? They seem real, don't they? These negative voices are another reason that you find yourself so stuck. You're listening to the negative messages, and playing that track over and over in your mind.

Some of my negative voices included: "Yeah, right, like you can do *that*!" "What makes you think you can get that or go there?" and, "Why are you even bothering? Others are so much better at this than you are!" These voices used to taunt me, and I believed them. Yet, by the standard definitions of monetary and professional "success," I had accomplished so much – more than I had ever dreamed possible. But these negative tracks continued to play – and I continued to beat myself up that I *should* be doing more, or I *should* be further ahead.

These voices are coming from your ego. Not your ego as in, "Ooh, I look amazing today," but rather your emotional ego – the side of you that often throws up roadblocks, and finds ways for you to stay stuck in what you're doing, because it is afraid of change.

That's not to say that the ego is a bad thing. On the contrary: it's often protecting us from something that might harm us, and that's a good thing. But when the ego is challenged by change, it doesn't like it. It gets scared, and it will try to stop us from moving forward, toward our dreams. It's where the fear or anxiety that we often experience comes from when we are confronted with change. It's where the *shoulds* come from. It's the source of the negative voices that question your dreams, and that question why you think you can do something, or why you deserve happiness or love.

You don't have to keep listening to your ego and playing that negative message track in your mind. In fact, you can switch tracks and listen to positive messages instead.

That other track – that other voice you can listen to – is your Real Self, your Higher Self, your Divine Self.

We all have this inner voice, but it may not be that loud. In fact, for some of us it can be very soft in the background, so we don't always pay attention to it. But, it's always there, and we can always access it. That track is the music of our true selves. Connecting with it and listening to it is the way that we find our way back – and it's how we get unstuck.

The ego and its negative voices are in our minds, and they can often parallel track with our subconscious inner programming of deeply held beliefs. The ego is driven by thought and logic – that's why it doesn't like change, because it has trouble processing the change and the reasons that it's happening.

But our Divine Self comes from the heart – it is guided by our feelings and our intuition. It's our emotional guide, and it gives us signals that are not difficult to interpret if we're paying attention. It's this simple: if it feels right to you, it is. If it doesn't feel right to you, it isn't. It's all about how you feel, and it's important to listen to this emotional guidance and not to disregard your feelings. The Divine Self is concerned with what is good for you and what you want, not what you *should* do or *should* want.

I know I often disregarded my feelings, because I was such a left-brain, logical thinker. In fact, my career in research deeply programmed this into me. I was taught early on that researchers don't *feel*. Instead, it was drilled into me that researchers can *know, believe,* and *recommend*, but they cannot *feel*. The professional culture in which I was immersed disregarded feelings or emotions. There was no time to waste on that "touchy-feely" stuff. We were only concerned with the tangible and measurable.

After spending fifteen years of my life in that world, no wonder I had completely disconnected from my Divine Self and my feelings as my guide. I was all up in my head trying to figure things out, and playing the negative ego track, when what I really needed to be doing was connecting to my heart space.

I'm not saying we should always be coming from our heart. Obviously, there is a role for logic and thinking in our lives. But, we need a balance. We need our Divine Self and intuition guiding us from our heart space, and we need our logical mind for action and daily activities. We need both to create a fully balanced and centered spirit. Otherwise, we're like the characters in the Wizard of Oz: the Tin Man with no heart, or the Scarecrow with no brain.

We all spend so much time in our heads that we often forget to listen to our hearts. Many of us are out of balance, between our heads and our hearts, without even knowing it. In my case, I didn't realize I had been operating primarily from my head, for pretty much my whole life, until just a few years ago.

Learning to feel after so many years of being disconnected was a new and weird place for me. Don't get me wrong. It's not as if I was a robot and didn't have relationships and love in my life. I did and I do. As I mentioned earlier, since my divorce, I have remarried. I love my husband, and we have a deep and powerful connection that is firmly rooted at the heart and soul level. I also have long-standing friendships that have stood the test of time and distance, simply because we are connected in our hearts.

But I wasn't listening to myself, to my emotions, to my body. I ignored all those personal feelings. I ignored all the signals and messages my Divine Self had sent. When I was frustrated with myself, my work, whatever – I would just grin and bear it, push even harder, and keep on going. Who had time to worry about how I felt, and all that "touchy-feely" stuff? I certainly didn't!

The fact is, it's *not* "touchy-feely" stuff. It is very real. Our Divine Self is ever present, and can communicate with us in several ways – if we're open to hearing the messages.

How do we listen to the positive music of our Divine Self? How do we embrace it? It's simple. We get quiet, and we ask ourselves questions. We simply go inwards and have a conversation with that deepest part of our heart and spirit. Asking questions is incredibly important. When you do this, instead of asking these questions of others around you, ask them of yourself, of your Divine Self.

You'll know you are talking to your Divine Self and not your ego, because your Divine Self is gentle and caring, and it comes to you when you ask it to. The ego is just running nonstop if you let it, and it comes in as that negative chatter. The ego doesn't need an invitation, but your Divine Self often does. It needs us to connect to it and to listen.

Our Divine Self is inside us metaphysically, but it also has a physical presence. It can talk to us in other ways if we are not going inwards to connect with it. If we are simply not communicating with our Divine Self at that level, it may send us signals using the physical realm – our bodies.

When our bodies are sick or not healthy, that's our Divine Self sending us a signal: trying to get our attention and get a message through to us. If we ignore that signal, the messages get bigger and louder.

Have you ever had an experience where you were just flat-out doing something or worrying about something and then, bam? You get injured, or you get really sick, and you are just out of commission? And, I mean really out of it, just unable to do anything. That is your Divine Self sending you the biggest signal it can: STOP! REST! STEP BACK! REBOOT! NOW!

As we look back on an episode like this, we might realize that we had been getting smaller messages before it happened. But, we ignored them and kept going, and we got what my life coach would describe as "the Mack truck experience," because we didn't respond to the softer messages. What she means is that we all get messages and signals from our Divine Self, but we often dismiss them. They start out light as a feather, but if we keep overlooking them, they increase in weight until we get the hit-by-a-truck experience where we're just laid up, flat on our back, with no choice but to listen. Even then, some of us still don't get it – we recover, and we go right back to life as it was before.

I injured my back on a work trip, but I ignored it and kept moving. It resulted in chronic back pain for years, and ultimately surgery. Yet the pain still lingered – and it would get stronger and more persistent when I felt stressed, or while I was traveling. In the last few years of my research career, when things were reaching an unbearable level of stuckness, I developed a constant tightness in my chest. I would call it the "bad butterflies," or the "anxiety butterflies." They would sometimes go down into my stomach, but usually they were in my chest. I would feel so tight at times that I could barely breathe. We are told to breathe deeply to relieve stress, but I couldn't even do that. I'd be gasping for that deep breath, and becoming even more stressed because I couldn't get it. It was a vicious circle.

Then there were the times when my chest and upper back would join forces to make me feel as twisted as a pretzel. The compression and tension were overwhelming. I used to wave it off, chalking it up to the physical toll of travel – getting on and off planes, lifting heavy bags, sleeping in hotel beds, constantly on the move. While all of that contributed to the pain I felt, it wasn't what was really going on.

My body was sending me messages. My Divine Self was trying to tell me something about what I was doing. I felt constricted and trapped in my body, and I also felt that way about my professional life at the time. But I didn't see this, and for a long time I didn't connect the dots about what these symptoms meant. On the outside, all looked good. I had made it to the top of my field, and I was making great money.

In part, that's why I stayed so long in that work and in that pain. I was following all of my *shoulds* and listening to my ego. I wasn't listening to my Divine Self – neither emotionally nor physically.

Those *shoulds* were the classic ones that so many of us live by, and that help keep us stuck. "My position is secure, so I *should* stay"; "I'm really good at what I do, so I *should* enjoy it"; "I am prospering financially, so I *should* keep going"; "I have had some real success, so I *should* keep building my book of business."

All of this was compounded by the biggest fear and *should* of all: "If I stop doing this, I don't know what I'll do – so I *should* just stick with it." Wasn't that perfect? By deciding to stick with something because I thought I *should*, I was creating a surefire way to keep myself stuck.

It's Your Turn:

Take a few moments to connect with your Divine Self. It's very simple. In fact, you've already started to do this by working through some of the exercises in this book! From now on, you're just going to become more aware of it, so that you can connect with your Divine Self any time you choose.

⌘ Get quiet; sit up straight with your feet on the floor and your arms and legs uncrossed. Close your eyes, and take those five slow, deep breaths to center yourself. Inhale through your nose, and exhale strongly through your mouth.
⌘ Go inwards.
⌘ Ask the questions you've always wanted answers to.
⌘ Then listen.
⌘ Just listen for the answers as your Divine Self comes to you and tells you what you already know, deep within you, in your heart.

Write down what you heard, and contemplate the answers. See how they fit with the things you listed earlier that you *want* in your life.

_____

_____

_____

_____

_____

Chapter 6

Time for Change:
The Reprogramming Process

I didn't connect with my Divine Self for a long time. I didn't understand the physical signals it was sending me until life got so unhappy, and I felt so run down, that I finally realized that *something* had to change.

I had just kept going for so long. I kept pounding along, moving to the next project, the next day, the next week – and pretty soon, life was just a blur. Was I really living? Even on weekends, I was often too tired and worn out to do anything of substance. I'd just flake out all day, trying to recharge. It would help, but it didn't fix anything. I started taking sleeping pills each weekend to make up for lost sleep during the week. These were all Band-Aid solutions.

I had a thriving career, but I was spending more and more time on the road and away from my husband. It made me miserable – the lonely hotel rooms, crowded airports, cramped airline seats. Waking up and not knowing what city I was in – only what time I needed to be at the airport for the flight to my next destination. I was in a constant state of sleep deprivation, and carrying tension and anxiety in my body. The work and the travel were a constant grind on me, at every level.

I couldn't take it any longer. My Divine Self finally got to me. The desire for something else became so great that it caused me to look at my life in new ways.

For me, that desire was to be at home, with my husband, who had survived cancer just a few years earlier. It was to spend my time doing something that had real value and meaning to me, and that helped other people. I kept asking myself, "What the hell am I doing, traipsing around the country, doing something that causes me stress and that no longer interests me?"

I was living Einstein's definition of insanity: doing the same thing over and over, and expecting different results. I knew deep down that something had to change. But I did what most of us do when change is needed: I resisted it. When we resist something, we just make it stronger so that whatever we focus on grows bigger. I became so focused on what I *didn't* want, instead of what I *did* want, and it made the situation even more insurmountable in my mind.

I couldn't see a way out. I would be leaving behind everything I had built during a decade with this firm, and now as a partner with my own book of business. I would leave to do what? I wasn't sure, but I thought all I needed to do was figure out a career change, and that would fix everything. That's when I started seeing a life coach and a career coach. I was laser-focused on figuring out the next career move. Once again, I was looking outside of myself for answers, and for a fix to the problem.

Of course, nothing really changed until I started looking within, working with my coaches to examine the difficult issues. Not by rehashing them or over-analyzing them, but simply by identifying what they were, understanding the long-held beliefs and inner programming behind them, and discovering where they came from. By gathering enough knowledge about them I could then release them – and move forward – to new beliefs and new programming.

It soon became apparent that while a career change may well have been where I was headed, it certainly wasn't the answer to everything I needed to address. Instead, the specifics of what a new career might be were put off to the side while I took time to dive deep, and look inside – to understand what was keeping me stuck and blocked. I realized that this was much bigger than my work.

Certainly, it seemed that most of my inner programming and long-held beliefs seemed to manifest primarily in my career, but I noticed that they were affecting other areas of my life, as well. Before a career change could happen, I had to address who I was, what my beliefs were, and what I needed to change within myself.

My first "aha" moment was simple but powerful in my transformational journey. I had uncovered the deeply held belief that I was not good enough. I had been desperately asking myself, and my life coach, "What if I'm not good enough, and what if my work isn't good enough? What if these beliefs are actually true?"

She stopped me in my tracks by asking, "What if you *are* good enough? What if your work *is* good enough?" All she did was turn the question on its head. It was a memorable moment, because it was so straightforward and so obvious – but I had never thought of it that way before. I came home that night and told my husband. He smiled and said, "Oh my goodness, you're just seeing that now? I've been saying this to you for years, and you're just getting it now?" I replied, "It's the skinny jeans, honey – I have to see it and believe it myself for it to resonate."

We all have those "aha" moments inside of us, just waiting to happen. Often, they are so simple that we wonder how we never even saw them before. But how can we, when we're running on a program that no longer serves us, and we're listening to the negative ego track? Some of us have never played a positive track in our minds, or connected to our Divine Self, so we don't know any better.

This is what the reprogramming is all about – changing the tune, and connecting to our inner guidance, our Divine Self, so that instead of hearing, "I'm not good enough," we start hearing, "I *am* good enough, just as I am."

When I first started my reprogramming work, I could only manage to replace "I'm not good enough" with "I'm good enough," instead of "I'm good enough, just as I am." I wasn't ready yet to step into the "just as I am" part. That seemed too far out of reach, because I had other underlying beliefs that were yet to be addressed. For example, I had deeply held beliefs that my worth as a person was about my work, or what I produced and achieved, rather than about me as a human being on the planet.

Some of the beliefs will have deeper roots than others. Some may seem to be too much of a stretch to reprogram at first. Go easy on yourself. Look for the beliefs with shallower roots, and start with what feels manageable. Then reach for the new, positive beliefs that you can handle and adopt.

Here's the really great thing about this system – once you know how to do it, you can go back anytime to modify or change the beliefs again. That's exactly what I did at a later date, once I had moved further along in my journey. I went back in and adjusted the belief to be "I am good enough, just as I am." It felt good, and I could welcome it. It was just the new and improved version of that particular belief.

Are you ready to begin reprogramming the long-held beliefs that no longer serve you? Are you ready to switch the tracks in your mind so that they are playing positive messages, and connecting to your Divine Self instead of your ego? Yes? Okay, let's do it!

It's Your Turn:

Sit in a comfortable place; somewhere you will not be disturbed for about fifteen minutes.

⌘ Get quiet; sit up straight with your feet on the floor and your arms and legs uncrossed. Close your eyes, and take your time with those five slow and deep breaths to center yourself. Inhale through your nose, and exhale through your mouth.

Think of a situation or pattern of behavior that keeps repeating in your life. You can use some of the situations you wrote about in earlier exercises, or you can pick something new. Now ask yourself these questions again, and write down the answers to each:

⌘ What is my underlying belief or perception about this situation?

⌘ What's driving that belief or perception?

⌘ Where does this belief come from? When or where did I learn it?

⌘ Is it truly my belief, or is it really someone else's belief?

⌘ Is it still a belief that works for me; is it serving my higher purpose? Or, is it something that was programmed in at an early age that no longer needs to be my story?

Make sure you are going inwards, and asking these questions of your Divine Self.

_____

_____

_____

_____

_____

Simply listen to what comes back – this is your Divine Self speaking to you and connecting with you. If you find that you have an underlying belief that is limiting, or no longer true, or no longer serving your higher purpose, the next step is to ask if you are ready to release that old belief and replace it with a new one, a better one, a positive one.

If you're not ready to release the old belief, you may need to do some more analysis on where it came from, and why you feel you need to hold on to it. You'll need to dig deeper on the driving force behind it, so that you can ultimately get to a point where you are ready to release it.

If you are ready to release the old belief, ask yourself what new program or positive belief might better serve you now, and into the future.

Be careful with this step. The new program has to be something you really *do* believe. Don't reach so far that you undermine your own valiant effort by creating a belief that is actually not believable to you. If you do that, you'll end up sabotaging yourself. So, close your eyes again and ask yourself:

⌘ What do I want to replace this long-standing belief with?
⌘ What works for me?
⌘ What do I want to hear in my mind that's a positive track?

_____

_____

_____

_____

_____

If you feel some resistance coming up around the new belief you chose, don't worry. What I mean by resistance is that when you say the new belief, you feel anxiety, fear, or doubt. Or, you might immediately hear the negative chatter track coming in from your ego. Either of these reactions is a signal that the new belief needs to be modified slightly, so that you can truly reprogram.

Acknowledge the resistance, accept it, and question where it's coming from. You may find that, like an onion, the beliefs you uncover have multiple layers to them. Just work on the top layer first, releasing it and replacing it with the new programming. Go easy on yourself, and work to find a slightly different version of the new belief that you can truly embrace at this time.

You may need to modify exactly what you are saying. For example, you may not be able to fully move from the old belief that "I never have enough money" to a new belief of "I always have plenty of money for anything I want." So, you could modify it by saying, "*I'm in the process of creating* plenty of money for anything I want." Or, you could say, "I always have *enough* money for *the things I need.*" Only *you* will be able to find the new belief that works for you at this time. Remember, you can always go back to this process to update and modify your new beliefs.

Once you have your new belief, and you can say it out loud without any reaction, look into a mirror and say it. Look directly into your own eyes, and say it out loud to yourself. See how it feels. Don't get distracted by your appearance, or whether your hair is combed. Look directly into your own eyes, and say the belief out loud. Send yourself love and compassion, and tell yourself that from now on, this is your belief; this is your new program that runs in your mind. I often find that it helps to put my hands over my heart when I say my new beliefs, so that I'm truly connecting and feeling it in my heart space.

Mirror work is extremely effective, and you'll see that many coaches and personal-development professionals incorporate it into their work. When I first started my journey, I pooh-poohed this, because I told myself I didn't have time, or I didn't feel like staring at myself in the mirror and talking to myself. Not to mention it just felt foolish to do so. The first few times I tried it, I felt so self-conscious. Even though no one was there to watch or hear me, I felt like such a dork. If you feel any of this, just know it's perfectly natural.

But, I can assure you that if you do it, mirror work is very powerful. You'll find that as you look into your own eyes, you can see if something isn't sitting right with you, or if fear, anxiety, or doubt is in there. If you just take a few minutes to work with your new beliefs in the mirror, you'll find that it helps you to connect more deeply with your Divine Self, in your heart and your spirit.

Essentially, in creating your new beliefs and saying them to yourself, you are developing your own affirmations. Some of you may have heard of or used affirmations at one point or another. They are positive statements that we repeat to ourselves throughout the day. Some people pin them up by their computer, or on mirrors, so that they see them regularly and are reminded of them. I am a firm believer in affirmations, but with one very big caveat: use them only if you really do *believe* them, and can embrace them. That's why I am so emphatic about the new beliefs you choose to reprogram.

You can read an affirmation and adopt it as your own – I often do this when I like something I hear, or when I read a statement that resonates with me. But, when you first start out with this work, creating your own affirmation carries more power and weight than adopting an affirmation that someone else may have written. You get to choose your own belief and your own affirmation. In doing so, you are beginning the journey of creating the life you truly want.

That might seem like a stretch – how does changing some beliefs equate to creating the life I truly want? Well, remember from earlier: our life is the outer reflection of what we believe and perceive on the inside. The program and beliefs you're running on have created your life up until now. You just may not have realized this, or even realized you had a program, but we all do. And, when we're not truly aware of what the program is, we're essentially running on autopilot.

This doesn't mean we don't make conscious choices in life – of course we do. You made a conscious decision to take the job you have right now, or to live in the home you have right now. Even when you feel as if you may not have had a choice, you did. We always have a choice. It's just that when we are running on autopilot, we don't see all the choices we have, and the choices we do make, are influenced by the deeply held beliefs running on that program in our subconscious.

That's why reprogramming our belief system is a key step on the road to transforming our lives. We have the choice to stay stuck in our old programming, or we can release it and move to a new and improved set of beliefs.

We can't create the life we want if we are unaware of the current beliefs, the existing program, and the choices we have made up to this point. Once we start reprogramming, we awaken to ourselves. It's as if we wake up from a long slumber of not paying attention to ourselves – and now we are opening our eyes, beginning to see things more clearly, and seeing them for what they are. We can create some space for new perspectives and creativity to come in.

Those old feelings of being stuck or anxious or frustrated start to subside. They are replaced with new feelings of courage, hope, and optimism. When we notice that we feel better, we know we are on the right path – because our emotions act as our internal compass, and they determine the energy we are emitting to the universe and to everyone around us.

Chapter 7
Energy Vibrations

We are all made up of energy. Everything in the world is vibrating at some energetic frequency – even inanimate objects, albeit with very slow vibrations.

We are emitting some level of energy all the time. Have you ever walked up to someone and just felt welcomed? Or, maybe you felt the opposite – they wanted to be left alone? That's because of the energy they are sending out, and what we are picking up from them.

Every single one of us is made up of these energetic frequencies. Our emotions, what we're thinking and feeling, are energy, and they determine our frequency or vibration. The vibrations we send out attract similar vibrations, reflecting back to us what we are thinking and feeling on the inside. This is the Law of Attraction at work.

Many of you may already be familiar with the Law of Attraction. For those of you who are not, it simply states that *like attracts like*. That is, whatever you send out you get back, like a boomerang. Some people also refer to this as karma. You can call it whatever you like, but it all comes down to energy: our energy, and the vibrations we're sending out to the universe.

Our emotions and energetic signals can be happening at high or low vibrations. When we are in a low-energetic vibration, we are often operating from a place of lack and anxiety. Lower-vibrating emotions include fear, despair, grief, powerlessness, unworthiness, guilt, insecurity, hatred, revenge, anger, discouragement, blame, worry, doubt, disappointment, overwhelm, frustration, pessimism, and boredom.

It's important to note that when we feel these emotions, they are not wrong or bad, and neither are we for feeling them. Remember, we are not about making ourselves wrong; we are about making ourselves right. So, when we have these feelings, it's important not to disregard them or condemn them. Instead, they need acknowledgement and acceptance. Ask yourself: is it okay to feel guilt, or fear, or whatever other emotion you're having right now? The answer to that question is always "yes." It's always okay to have a feeling. Be in acceptance for what you are feeling – don't dismiss it.

Feelings aren't actions, and they don't harm us physically – unless we bottle them up and don't acknowledge them. When we do that, we start creating harm, because these lower-level emotions begin eating away at our insides. They keep us vibrating in a low-level place, where we can get stuck and have trouble moving out. They start having a physical impact on our body – showing up in many different ways. Toward the end of my long career in research, the stress of constantly operating from lower-vibrating emotions manifested physically in my lower and upper back, and in my chest. The tension I used to carry in these areas was often unbearable – until I was able to address the source of it all.

Acknowledge your emotions, allow yourself to feel them, and ask where they're coming from. Find out what's driving them, and whether a belief or thought needs to be changed – so that you can change what you are feeling.

Often, we look at situations and we feel pain because of them. Or, rather, we *think* we feel pain because of them. Take my divorce, for example. I was in a lot of pain, feeling grief, shame, anxiety, and depression about getting divorced. But, was it the actual divorce that caused that? No, that was a legal procedure that was relatively straightforward. What caused the pain and suffering was my perception of the situation. I viewed divorce as a shameful and embarrassing thing – as do many people in our society. My perception of what I thought about the situation, and what I thought I *should* be doing, meant that I felt many of these lower-level emotions, and I kept myself stuck on that end of the emotional scale.

On the other end of the spectrum, there are the higher-vibrating emotions: contentment, hopefulness, optimism, courage, passion, happiness, joy, freedom, love, and enlightenment. Courage is the point at which things start to become unstuck. Courage is where we reach the place that we're ready and willing to make changes. We recognize that we have to step into the new, and leave some of the old behind. It takes courage to go through the reprogramming process – to go deep into our subconscious, examine the old beliefs, release them, and replace them with new beliefs.

When we feel these higher-level emotions, we are vibrating at a higher frequency: a frequency that's like a radio signal transmitting to the universe. The universe responds by matching these vibrations and frequencies. When we are vibrating low, the universe will match that signal and bring us more of it. Ever heard the saying, "Misery loves company"? If we are vibrating at a higher frequency, the universe recognizes that and matches it, thus the saying, "Success begets success." These are just other ways of expressing the Law of Attraction – whatever we send out we get back.

So, when we are down and feeling sorry for ourselves, we won't attract the beautiful and wondrous things we want into our lives. We are stuck in a low vibration, and until we raise it, we won't receive anything different from what we usually do. Similarly, if we're in a higher vibration, we may be astounded by how fast we create and attract things to us. It's because we're sending out the signal that we're open, ready to receive, accepting and grateful for our situation, and eager for more good to come to us.

The great thing about energy is that although we cannot see it, we can feel it – and we can work with it. We're not restricted to the emotions or vibrations we're feeling at any given time. We have a choice to change them, just as we can change our thoughts and underlying beliefs. We can choose to feel gloomy and see the suffering in a situation, or we can choose to feel better and find the good that's coming from the situation. These are choices we make every day.

Often we default into seeing the bad in a situation, and staying at that low vibration. Why do we do that when we know that being in a higher vibration leads to better things for us, and for everyone around us? The reason is that we are playing small. Being small, being hidden, is often our safe spot. If we don't stick our neck out and dare to pursue our dreams and desires, we get to feel comfortable and secure – even if that means we remain fearful or anxious.

This doesn't mean we have to pretend to be happy about something when we're not. In fact, it's quite the opposite. When we have a low-vibrating emotion, we need to acknowledge that emotion and truly feel it. Once we allow the emotion to just be there, we can then start to question if it's our truth – so we can release it, and make a choice to raise our vibration.

It's Your Turn

Think about how you usually feel:

⌘ Do you usually go through your days feeling higher- or lower-vibrating emotions?

⌘ If you're often feeling some of the lower-level emotions, acknowledge that they are there; accept them for what they are.

⌘ Question why these emotions are there. Are they your truth? Do you have to stay in these emotions, or could you raise your vibration?

⌘ Remind yourself that you have a choice. You can dwell in the lower-level emotion or you can release it, choose a different perspective, and look for the good.

⌘ Can you reach for a new thought, perception or belief that brings you to a higher-vibrating emotion?

⌘ How does it feel? What is that better thought? What emotions do you have as you think it?

_____

_____

_____

_____

_____

Do you notice your energy vibration rising as you consciously choose more positive thoughts and emotions? When we're aware of our thoughts and emotions, we can decide to change them, to shift our vibration, and to create a more positive world for ourselves.

Chapter 8
Releasing the Past and the Negative

As we reprogram our beliefs, raise our energetic vibration, and start to look forward with hope, many of us still look back on our past. We may remember experiences that make us cringe. We may feel shameful about some of the things we have done or said. But, the past has happened. We cannot have a do-over. We can simply use the past to learn, and then move forward. Yet, when we keep wallowing in it, allowing the pain and scars from the past to linger and remain embedded, we never truly address them. And this contributes to our feeling stuck. As part of our process of getting unstuck, we have to learn to let go of the past, to release it.

Just as we looked at our inner programming, we must also look at what we're still bottling up and holding inside. This takes courage. Maybe we are still angry for wrongs done to us. Maybe we feel wracked with guilt because of a wrong that we did to someone else. We have to recognize and acknowledge the emotions we are storing inside, so that we can release them and move beyond them. Without release of these lower-vibrating feelings, we do not get to move on. We stay stuck.

But how do we release them? Easier said than done, right? Yes. But it's not so difficult that you can't do it. To release those pent-up emotions, we have to look deeply into what they are. We have to use a process that is similar to our reprogramming. We connect with our Divine Self and ask questions, listening for the answers that are already within us.

- ⌘ Why do I feel the way I do?
- ⌘ What's the source of my hurt?
- ⌘ Does it still need to be true today?
- ⌘ What's more important? Holding on to the past, and the emotions that are eating away at me inside? Or, releasing them – exhaling them out of my body, and releasing them forever?

This is a vital step in getting unstuck. For without surrender to a feeling or an emotion, it will be stuck inside us until we are able to move it out. And, you are the only one who can move it out – not anyone else. Here again, we often look to the outside to fix how we're feeling. We want another person to complete us or to fill the emptiness. But, as you know by now, it's not about *them*; it's about *you*. You have more power and strength than you ever thought possible. It's all inside you.

Now, you might read that and think, well, how can it be all about me when that person is in the wrong, and they are the one who caused me hurt? How can that be all about me, and why should I surrender the pain and angst that I feel?

Well, it's the Law of Attraction at work again. Remember, the vibrations that we send out attract similar vibrations, and those vibrations are the reflection of what we are thinking and feeling on the inside.

Take our earlier example where we may feel disrespected; that someone in our life is not giving us the respect we think we deserve. This may cause us to feel angry, or resentful, or hurt. But, when we take a moment to ask, "Am I respecting myself?" Chances are, the answer is that we're not. And, if we're not respecting ourselves, then others won't respect us, either.

As we do our inner reprogramming, and we start listening to the positive tracks in our minds, we are sending ourselves love and compassion. We are recognizing our own feelings and emotional needs. In creating this positive energy from within, we are sending out the same energetic signal to the universe. We have always been sending out a signal. It's just that the old signal may have been one that said, "I don't respect myself."

Now the signal is going to change, and be, "I fully respect myself." In changing our program, we'll start attracting more respectful relationships into our lives; and those who were disrespectful will start to drift away. As we do this, we are releasing the lower-vibrating emotions, the blame, and the resentment.

Let them go – for we no longer need the other person to satisfy a need, or to behave in a certain way, for us to feel respected. We respect ourselves, so we don't need to rely on others' respect. As we release the need for respect from others, and instead we feel it within, our vibration shifts to a higher energy frequency, and we begin to attract the respect we had been looking for all along. But this can't happen unless we have already reprogrammed our belief, and we are already releasing the lower-vibrating emotions.

Some people hear this and roll their eyes: "Yeah, right! How did I create this crappy situation for myself? And why should I be the one to change?" Or maybe they have actually tried to use the Law of Attraction in their lives, but have not had any results.

I understand this. I was skeptical about it all at the beginning, too. I thought I was practicing it, but I was seeing very few results. Or, my results were spotty – some things would happen and others would not. I couldn't quite figure out if it really was working. And, that's when I hit on the missing pieces: accepting, allowing, and receiving.

When we identify situations that bother us, and we understand the feelings and the underlying beliefs behind them, we have to first accept it all as it is. Accept it. You may not like it, you may not enjoy feeling disrespected or not loved enough. But just accept that this is how you feel. Remember, these are just feelings. And as you've already discovered: thoughts, feelings, and beliefs can all be changed.

It's only when we recognize, acknowledge, and accept our feelings that we can then move forward in releasing them – and exhaling them out of us. We can begin to forgive ourselves and others; we can identify if an underlying belief is part of the issue; we can assess if we need to reprogram it.

It's Your Turn:

Try practicing acceptance and release of lower-vibrating emotions.

⌘ Think of a situation where you are holding onto blame or resentment.

⌘ Just allow yourself to feel the emotion, even if it feels difficult or uncomfortable at first. Remind yourself that the feeling cannot hurt you; it's just a feeling and it can be changed.

⌘ Take a deep breath in, and as you exhale just drop into the emotion. Just breathe into it.

⌘ Remember to keep breathing. Take deep breaths, in and out, as you allow yourself to fully engage in this feeling.

⌘ Say to the feeling, "I acknowledge you. I feel your presence. I know you are there."

⌘ Now, thank the feeling. Yes, you read that correctly. Thank the feeling, for the feeling is a message for you. It's a signal for you to pay attention. Thank the feeling for coming into your life, so that you might better understand yourself.

_____

_____

_____

_____

_____

Now, still breathing deeply and with your eyes closed, ask yourself:

- ⌘ What is the underlying thought or belief behind this feeling?
- ⌘ Ask if the belief needs to be reprogrammed, and if you can release the lower-vibrating emotion.
- ⌘ Listen for the answer, and acknowledge it.
- ⌘ Now, exhale deeply and release the feeling by saying, "Thank you for being here, but I no longer need to feel this way. I release this feeling – and I replace it with love."

_____

_____

_____

_____

_____

You can repeat this releasing exercise any time you feel those lower-vibrating emotions come up. They are not bad, and they are not wrong. They are messages and signals that guide our well-being. If we acknowledge them, we no longer need to hold on to them. We are telling them we understand why they are here. They have served their purpose, and we can now release them – so that we can release ourselves from the negative, stuck place in which they hold us hostage.

Chapter 9

Embracing the Positive
and the Possibilities

We have to be in a place of allowance, and open to receiving, for good things to come to us – whether those are relationships, material objects, a new career, or some other situation. Without this allowing piece, we block ourselves from receiving. And, that allowing is part of our inner programming.

If we are programmed to think we are not worthy or deserving of love, then it is unlikely we will ever receive it, because we're not allowing it into our lives. Even if we put it out there that we want to manifest our perfect job or our soul mate, and we get really specific about the qualities each should have, we won't get it unless we believe we can – *and* we allow it to happen.

This is why the foundational principles of reprogramming our inner beliefs and raising our vibration are so incredibly important. These processes are not just about changing how we think about ourselves and our lives; they also put us in a place of allowing, so that we are ready to receive the amazing life we want to create for ourselves.

Being Open to Receive

We can only receive what we allow ourselves to have. If we are in resistance to what we say we want, or we are in resistance to receiving it, we will not create or manifest it.

This was a big one for me. I've been independent for pretty much my whole adult life. Even when I got married the second time around and knew better, I would rarely ask for help when I needed it. In fact, my husband would often be exasperated with me. Instead of allowing him to help me in even the simplest way, such as lifting grocery bags, I would often breeze on by, carrying all of them myself, although he was right there and willing to do it.

It was the same in my career. I had a difficult time learning to delegate, to trust others with the work I was doing. I often pushed myself to the breaking point before finally admitting that I needed help, and that I should be handing off to my team some of the tasks I was doing. I had a team, but I wasn't always giving them everything they could be working on because I felt it would get done faster and easier if I just did it myself.

I know I am not alone in this. Many of us are closed off from receiving, particularly career-driven women. We feel we have to give, give, give, and we do it all to prove we are good enough. Not only that, but we have to do it without help. We're playing the role of super hero. Doing everything to perfection singlehandedly is our super power. That's all great, except for one flaw – it's ridiculous.

There is a flow of giving and receiving. If we close ourselves off to receiving, we're disturbing the natural order of things. We all need help, and we all have to learn how to accept help. Accepting is an important part of the give-and-receive flow, yet so many of us don't do it. We don't get it that receiving is a good thing. For those of you who feel that accepting help means being a burden to others, or showing weakness, here's a newsflash: most people want to offer their help, their time, their expertise.

Most people want to give to others and contribute in a meaningful way. If we're not open to receiving this help, then we're closing off the flow in the cycle. If we mess with the flow of giving and receiving, we're out of balance, and we create blocks that can keep us stuck, unable to receive.

Asking for What We Want

Similar to being open to receive, and the next step in the process, is actually *asking for* what we want or need. Again, so many of us don't actually ask for help or for what we want. But, if we don't ask, how will anyone – including the universe – *know* what we want? We are taught in many ways in our society, and across so many religions, the basic tenet, "Ask and you shall receive." It permeates our life – both metaphysically and physically. When we want to make changes or create something in our lives, the critical starting point is to ask for it, and to ask for it with detail and clarity.

The universe is always working for us, not against us. But it cannot deliver what we want if we are not asking. It also cannot deliver what we want if our subconscious programming is asking for something different. Even when we get clear on what we want, and we align our conscious and subconscious desires so they are working together, we need to be detailed about what it is we want or the direction we want to take.

If we are vague in what we ask from the universe, then vagueness is what we'll get back. Or we'll get something that satisfies the basic request, but differs from what we had hoped for. It's the same as giving someone a project with incomplete instructions or ambiguous directions, and then wondering why the final product is not to our liking. How can we expect it to come back with clarity and precision, if we don't provide the proper details and guidelines?

We may be dissatisfied in our work, and ask the universe to bring us a new job opportunity. That's the basic principle in asking for what we want. But, if we don't provide a real description of what that new job should be – how much we want to get paid, the position or the field in which we want to work, where we want to work, how long our commute should be, and so on – the universe may well deliver us a new job opportunity, but it might not look anything like what we actually wanted.

We have to ask for what we want; we have to make sure our inner programming is aligned with it and open to receive; and we have to be very specific about what we want or the new direction we wish to take. This is true whether we are asking the universe for something, or asking another person for some help.

Forgiveness and Acceptance

We also have to take the time to forgive, to release judgment and criticism. When we hold a grudge or blame someone for something, we're actually locking it all into place. We're locking their behavior into place, and we're locking into place the energy that's needed to hold that grudge.

Holding grudges or being angry will keep us in a low-energetic vibration, and unable to move beyond it, because we have become so consumed by the hatred or the outrage we feel. Rest assured that the person we are holding a grudge against is not expending the same amount of energy we are. Even if they have remorse for what happened, it's not the same type of energy that *we're* focused on in holding that grudge.

The same goes for blame and judgment and criticism. We are so quick to point the finger and say, "I would never do that," or "I can't believe he did that," or "Why the heck would she think that?" We are swift to pass judgment or to find fault – and we often do it without any context for the situation or the people involved. But, in doing this, again we lock the behavior we're judging or criticizing into place, and we end up seeing only the bad and not the good. Remember, when we point a finger, there are three pointing right back at us.

Indeed, many of the things we get upset about, we do ourselves all the time. Do you ever get mad at someone cutting you off in traffic, and say that you never do that? Think again. When was the last time you cut in front of someone or forgot to turn on your blinker? Often, some of the things that push our buttons the most are the things we do ourselves. We're so outraged by them that we don't stop to ask if we really do these things, too. If we recognize that we do, it immediately diffuses our anger and releases the frustration. We can no longer hold the other person in contempt without holding ourselves accountable.

Criticism is another tough one. Ever find yourself just pointing out the bad things, the defects, the problems? We all do this, and in some cases, we're actually trained to do it. During my research career, I was often tasked with identifying the areas for improvement and the problems that needed to be fixed. Of course, corporations need to understand the weaknesses in their brand or their product, and that's what I would do for them. But, when we only focus on what's bad, we often bypass what is good.

When we only present the critique of a given situation, those who are involved become deflated, since they are only being told what is wrong. It's the same in relationships. How does your partner or friend or co-worker respond when you point out their flaws, or continuously find fault with their behavior?

I mentioned acceptance earlier, but let's come back to it for a moment because it goes hand in hand with forgiving and finding the good. It's important to realize that we don't have to condone someone or something in order to accept it. For example, I don't condone suicide, but I accept that it happens. It is something that happens in life, and we may not like it, but we can accept that it is so. When we can accept things for what they are, we also gain the power to change them. For without first accepting what is, we cannot move beyond that place – and we end up stuck.

Forgiveness and acceptance help us get unstuck. These acts remove some of the blocks that stop us from getting where we want to go, and help us get to that important allowing place. Instead of judging others and picking them apart, try instead to simply accept them for who they are. As long as you are judging or criticizing them, you are locking that situation or behavior into place.

Other people energetically sense our judgment, and it puts them on the defensive. If we can just accept them for who they are, we actually release both parties. We get released from our low-vibrational feelings of disapproval, criticism and being blocked from moving ahead, and the other person is also released from our judgment. That doesn't mean we are letting them get away with something, for they still have to live with whatever they may have done. But, we are choosing to release ourselves from the situation so that *we* may move on.

Gratitude

This leads me to another significant component to include in our journey of personal development: gratitude. As we replace judgment and criticism with acceptance and forgiveness, we can build even further to regularly practice gratitude.

Gratitude is often discussed in personal-development circles, and for good reason. Gratitude is one of the highest-vibrating emotions. When we are in gratitude we are in an allowing space, and we are open to receiving. We are sending out a signal to the universe saying that we appreciate what we have – and that we're ready for more. There is real power in practicing gratitude daily.

Personally, I have made it my daily habit to share with others, out loud, when I see beauty in the world and I feel grateful for something. I also do what many others practice as well – journaling on gratitude. It doesn't have to be a long journal entry – just listing three to five different things each day for which you are grateful can make a big difference.

The process and habit of doing this trains us to look for the good. So that instead of looking for the bad things, we now look for different things each day that are good, and for which we are thankful and blessed. As we practice this gratitude, it reinforces our inner program of positive beliefs and our outer program of interfacing with the world around us. We move out of that place of judgment, criticism, and making things wrong, and into a space where good things and blessings are a daily part of life.

I can hear some of you saying, "Three to five different things a day? That's a lot!" Is it, really? If you're having trouble with that, just think of people around the world and in your own communities who don't have anywhere near what you have. Sometimes we need to remember the basics. We may take the roof over our heads for granted, but if we stop and think about it, we find that we feel grateful to have a place to live and call our home. It can be that simple.

It's your turn:

Pause for a moment, and think of someone or something that you've been finding fault with recently.

- ⌘ Take a moment to stop those negative thoughts – just put a pin in them for now.
- ⌘ Take a deep breath, and think about that person or situation again.
- ⌘ Now, find five positive things to say about them or it.

_____

_____

_____

_____

_____

How do you feel now when you see the good in people or situations? Do you feel better or worse? We can't help but feel better when we look for the good things in life. And, the beauty of feeling better is that we are raising our energy vibration so that we move into a space of allowing and acceptance.

Spend a whole day not judging anyone or anything, and work your way up to a whole week of it.

- ⌘ The moment you hear that judging thought in your head, or you start speaking it out loud, stop yourself in your tracks.

⌘ Simply say, "Stop. This is a judgment-free zone."
⌘ Now, find something positive to say about the person or situation.
⌘ Journal on how difficult it was to do, and how you felt afterwards, when you were able to stop the judgment and replace it with positive thoughts and feelings. You might also count how many times you catch yourself judging people or situations.

_____

_____

_____

_____

_____

We are all susceptible to judging others, but the trick is to notice it, stop it, and replace it with something positive. Just as we can reprogram our thoughts and beliefs about ourselves, we can also reprogram our thoughts and beliefs about others.

Get a journal, and record three to five things daily for which you are grateful.

⌘ Each day, record different things than the day before.
⌘ Do this with a partner, or have your family do it with you, and compare with each other your daily offerings of gratitude.

Start right now in the space provided below.

_____

_____

_____

_____

_____

When we practice gratitude regularly, we cannot help but feel better. It expands our love, our acceptance, and our allowing, so that we may be open to receive even more.

Chapter 10

Clearing the Mind;
Finding White Space to Create

Y ou may be feeling some resistance towards some of the things I'm describing in this personal-transformation process. You may be thinking, "Gee, this is a lot of work. I have to start reprogramming myself, changing my perceptions of others, practicing forgiveness and gratitude, and giving up any judgment and criticism?" It's true – this may seem like a lot to begin with. But how can you move towards the life you want if you don't make the changes that are needed? If you didn't have to do much to change, you wouldn't be reading this book right now – and you wouldn't be wondering about how to get unstuck.

The processes we've covered may be challenging at first, but they form the necessary foundation from which we can build the life we want. Once we have begun this inner work, our minds and hearts move more into balance, and we find that the necessary space opens up for us to envision what it is that we really want – and how we might get there.

As I went through these processes, I found that some white space in my head and heart started to open up. Suddenly, I was having thoughts that never occurred to me before – simple but powerful thoughts. I was able to start thinking about what life might be like if I really could create what I want, and move toward my life purpose. And instead of the ego chatter immediately coming in, there was room to breathe, to really contemplate the possibilities.

Before I did all the reprogramming and started shifting my energy vibrations, the ability to find that white space and start bringing some clarity into my life was just not there. I couldn't see past what my life was in that moment, and I was unable to clear my mind to allow bigger, more creative, truly exciting thoughts to happen. All those years, I had yearned for the big breakthrough – but it was all for naught, because I was not in a space of allowing and openness.

In reprogramming our deeply held beliefs, and switching to the positive tracks of our Divine Self instead of the negative ego chatter, we're focusing on bringing the conscious and subconscious minds into alignment. We are also connecting to our heart, and we're listening to our inner guidance about which beliefs are true for us and serve our higher purpose. Only our heart can truly understand this – it's beyond the realm of our mind. Our heart tells us that we deserve more love, compassion, and respect. We may know this in our mind, but until we feel it in our heart, it doesn't resonate fully in our subconscious.

As we feel ourselves opening up to new possibilities, and the white space to create begins to show itself, there are some techniques we can use to enhance the process and bring us even more clarity.

Meditation

Part of getting unstuck and shifting our beliefs is rooted in clearing the mind. So many of us have what some people refer to as "monkey mind" – we have a bunch of different thoughts racing through there at any given time. Often, these thoughts run the range of our to-do list. "Gotta get this done, call that person, finish up that email, order that book, call the cable company…" – the list goes on and on. Busy parents, especially, can relate to this – not only does the list include you, but it's dominated by all the various needs of your kids as well.

We do clear our minds and find some white space when we work through our reprogramming. But we may not be reprogramming daily, or excavating very deeply each day on our inner beliefs. So, we need a frequent, convenient, and easy way to clear our minds. Meditation is a helpful tool to do just that.

I know that when I first thought about meditation, I imagined hippies sitting around for hours doing nothing and being totally unproductive. You might say that I had an unfavorable and skeptical view about the purpose of meditation and about the notion of incorporating it into my life. You would be right. But I am now a firm believer in the practice.

I decided to give it a try in my efforts to be open-minded about the various techniques I could employ to help me live a happier, more fulfilled life. At first, it felt weird and awkward, and seemed like a big waste of time. I was just sitting there doing nothing, and trying to be engaged in the meditation track or the belief statement on which I was to meditate. But I persisted. If there's one thing I've learned across all my experiences, it's that you have to give something a fair chance before deciding if it's right for you.

On the second day, I felt the same, and again on the third. Then on the fourth day, I found I was better able to stay in my seated posture and focus on the meditation. If I found my mind wandering off, I just followed what the instructor said, and I brought my attention back to my breathing. Having had trouble with breathing in recent years, I was thrilled to discover that the calmness of the process brought me results as I learned to breathe more deeply and rhythmically.

The big breakthrough came about two weeks into my endeavor. I found I was coming back from meditating with a clear mind and a refreshed sense of self. I would set aside the same time every morning to meditate. I would do it right after I got up and walked my dog, and before I did anything else. I found that it made me feel more alive, more awake, and more ready for the day ahead. Sitting down to review email and work seemed less stressful than before, and I didn't have this perpetual rush of anxiety about getting things done. Instead, there was more calmness and serenity floating about me in the mornings, and I approached each task with greater focus and productivity. It felt good. I had to admit it: this meditation thing works!

I am by no means a master of meditation. But I have experienced its impact first hand, and I highly recommend it. To those of you who are skeptics, I hear you loud and clear – and I appeal to your wisdom to try it every day for three weeks and see what happens. You don't have to do it for long – ten to fifteen minutes is all it requires. If that's too long at the beginning, just do five minutes. Just do what feels right for you, and what you can manage. Then build to longer times as you get used to the process. Try a guided meditation, or pick one of your new belief affirmations that you developed during the reprogramming process, and meditate on it.

The benefit of a clear mind and a calm energy field is that we gain power in that state. We are able to quiet the "monkey mind," and to center and ground ourselves toward a place of serene strength – where anything seems and is entirely possible.

Being the Observer

Meditating is great for calming, for clearing the mind, for setting our intentions. But, we may still find ourselves in situations where the clarity and calmness are not present. We may be flustered with work requirements, or dealing with demanding clients or bosses. We may be having a disagreement with a loved one or friend.

At these times, it's helpful to take a deep breath and slip into observer mode. What this means is to simply start observing yourself in the given situation, how you are feeling and behaving. If another person is involved, observe how they are reacting to you. We can learn a lot from taking on this observer role. It allows us to step out of the heat of the moment, and to see things for what they really are.

For example, let's say you're engaged in a difficult conversation in the workplace, where your boss or a client is pressing you to deliver something in a very short timeline. They are stressed, and so are you – there are a lot of demands. You may be finding yourself on the defensive, and feeling put upon. If we slip into observer mode, we can see what may really be going on with the other person and with ourselves. The other person may be under pressure from someone higher up, and they are vibrating that anxious energy in our direction. Or, perhaps we are holding resentment toward the other person because this type of thing happens all the time. So maybe that means something is going on with us – we may be allowing the other person to press us for deliverables because we're really pressing ourselves.

When we take on that observer role, we begin to see the energetic dynamics of our feelings and behavior, and those of others. We start to see what's going on inside, and it helps us identify if there are beliefs or thought patterns that are no longer serving us, or that need to be adjusted. It can also help us modify our reactions or behavior right there in the moment. If we see that our client or boss is simply emitting anxiety, we can take steps to calm that and diffuse the situation, rather than escalating it.

I also use the observer technique when I find my ego and Divine Self locked in a tennis match of thoughts. This can happen when I'm working through some reprogramming. The ego will send all kinds of thoughts and messages to keep me stuck in an old belief, while my Divine Self wants me to move to a new belief that will better serve my higher good. Sometimes this process can feel like a bit of a struggle. However, if I take on the role of observer and simply watch the tennis match, it helps release the resistance and allows me to let go of the ego thoughts or lower-vibrating emotions.

When I do this, I find myself looking at the ego and saying to it, "Oh, these thoughts again? When are we going to be done with these? This is so tedious, and this track is so old!" I can only realize these things when I am in observer mode: when I have taken a step back, and I'm observing my thoughts at play with one another. As I see them for what they are, the ego thoughts just become boring and tiresome, rather than being a voice that can command fear and attention. At the same time, I am also seeing thoughts coming from my Divine Self for what they are: benefiting my higher good, and taking me to higher-vibrating emotions of courage, hopefulness, optimism, joy, and freedom.

Setting Boundaries and Learning to Say No

This is an important technique to help us in our personal-development journey, and we can use it in every aspect of our lives. Often, we find ourselves stretched, or constantly saying "yes" to requests when what we really want to do is say "no." We may feel some sense of obligation to whoever is asking. But, the fact is that when we say yes and we really mean no, we take ourselves out of alignment – the outer self is saying one thing, but the inner self is feeling and vibrating with different thoughts and emotions.

As we seek to align our inner beliefs and thoughts with what we do outwardly, it's important to set boundaries and learn to say "no." This doesn't mean we are rude to people who ask things of us. Rather, it's about taking a step back before answering the request. As we take a moment to consider it, we may ask ourselves some questions: Is this something I truly want to do? Is it a priority for me; do I have time? Does it serve my higher good?

If the answer to these questions is "yes," then the answer to the request is a simple "yes." But, if the answer to any of the questions is "no," then we may want to sit with the request for a while before responding. Take the time to assess if we really want to engage. We can simply say we'll think about it, and get back to that person a little later. This provides some space to consider the request, rather than offering an immediate response, which can often be a knee-jerk reaction.

Many of us are afraid to say no. We worry we won't be liked, or we won't be respected, or some other concern. But, if we're saying yes for these reasons, we're operating from a place of lack and fear, instead of a place of abundance and love. We're being hard on ourselves, making ourselves do things that we may not want to, because we're scared of what might happen.

In some instances, we may feel we just can't say no because we have a difficult boss or supervisor. We may look at a situation at work and feel that we don't have any control or choice. But, look again. There are always choices and ways to navigate differently. The first step is being aware of what is really going on. Use your observer mode to assess the energetic dynamic at play. Then consider what you may be able to change. Remember, you do have control over the way you perceive the situation, or how you behave. Is there a way you can work around this situation? Is there a new boundary you may be able to implement? It could be as basic as always taking your lunch break or always getting some fresh air during the day so you feel more refreshed and better equipped to handle the situation. We always have choices about boundaries. Even if the boundaries we choose are small and simple, they can still make a big difference.

During my years of being a partner in a research firm, I had many clients with many demands, often pressuring me on timelines and deliverables. I would say yes because I thought I had to; because if I didn't, the client might no longer work with me or might no longer value my services. However, in saying yes to everyone else, I was saying no to myself. I ended up working around the clock to meet everyone else's needs, while my own were going unmet. I was exhausted and burned out, and it led to resentment.

Then I started setting some simple boundaries: I no longer answered emails or phone calls after 7 pm unless it was an emergency. I stated realistic timelines for projects. I blocked parts of my day for personal growth and physical exercise, instead of letting all my time get usurped by endless work and conference calls. I started bundling my business trips into specific days and dates to consolidate time spent at home.

When I started doing these simple things, I was fearful of how my clients might react. It was a lot of angst over nothing. In virtually every case, they accepted the terms I began working with. All it took was for me to finally respect my own time and my own needs, set my boundaries, abide by them, and start using the word "no." In doing this, I was giving myself the compassion and love I deserved, and it meant that others around me started doing the same.

Separating Needs from Wants

We touched on this earlier when we looked at all the *shoulds* we impose on ourselves, and that we hear from our ego. As we practice some of these everyday techniques of being the observer and learning to say no, it's also helpful to be aware of whether we're doing something because a need is driving it, or whether it's something we truly want.

Are we agreeing to take something on because we *need* to prove we can do it, or we *need* the respect from someone else, or we *need* to show off our skills? Or, are we taking something on because we want to, because we have the time, and because it fits with what we'd like to be doing in our lives?

Remember to look at whether you're approaching a situation from a place of *should* and *need,* rather than *want* and *would like to.* There is a difference – and the way to distinguish is by tapping into your emotions. How you feel about someone, something, or the whole situation is your guide. Your feelings will let you know if the situation is in alignment with who you truly are.

If we are in need, then we are usually in a lower-level energy vibration, looking to other people or things to meet this need and using situations to try to satisfy it. Often, we feel discouraged or frustrated or depressed in this place. If we are in alignment and we want or desire to do something, then our energy vibration will be higher. We will feel hopeful or optimistic or joyful or fulfilled.

If you find yourself *needing* or *shoulding*, take a look at what's going on below the surface. Is there a limiting perception or belief that can be released and reprogrammed? Can you identify what you would *want*, instead? Can you allow yourself to accept that, and move into it, leaving the *needs* and *shoulds* behind? Be aware of your energy and your emotions, and use the reprogramming process to help you separate the needs from the wants.

From Chaos to Clarity

Area of My Life: _____

	What I Want To Change			What I Want This Area Of My Life To Be	
What I Don't Want	Why	How It Makes Me Feel	What I Do Want	Why	How I Want To Feel When I Have It

Chapter 11
Creating the Life You Want

N ow that we have the key elements in place, let's build the life you want. You've begun reprogramming, you're letting go of lower-vibrating emotions, you're raising your energetic vibration, you're allowing and desiring the positive, and you have some techniques to help open up space for clarity and creativity. You're prepared now to evaluate and embark on the life you want to create.

If you're still feeling as though you don't know exactly what you want, don't worry. We'll start with the basics, and with what is often the easiest thing to get clear on: what we don't want. When we're able to identify what we *don't* want, it helps bring us clarity about what we *do* want.

It's Your Turn:

Identify all the things that bother you about your life. What do you wish you could change?

⌘ Take ten sheets of paper, turn them sideways, and write one area of your life at the top of each page:
   – Career/Work
   – Financial/Money
   – Family
   – Relationships

- Social/Friends
- Health/Physical Well-Being
- Community
- Spirituality
- Personal Growth
- Mental/Emotional Well-Being

⌘ Draw six columns down the page as shown on page 96. On the left-hand side, above the first three columns, write: "What I Want to Change," and label the three columns under that with "What I Don't Want," "Why," and "How It Makes Me Feel." On the right-hand side, above the next three columns, write "What I Want This Area Of My Life To Be," and label the three columns under that with "What I Do Want," "Why," and "How I Want To Feel When I Have It."

⌘ Take one page, with one area of your life, and start on the left-hand side. Start listing out the things that bother you, the things you don't want, and the things you want to change in that area of your life.

⌘ For each item on the list, fill in the next two columns: *why* you don't want this in your life anymore, and how it makes you *feel* right now. Just let it all out – it can be incredibly cathartic to do this. Take deep breaths as you do it, and exhale powerfully to fully release all that pent-up emotion.

⌘ Once you have completed all three columns on the left-hand side of the page, it's time to pivot and go to the right-hand side. Go line by line, and as you look at what you *don't* want, start creating its opposite mate: what you *do* want. So, based on what you don't want, identify what you do want. (Remember, not what you think you *should* want, but what you *do* truly want.)

⌘ Now, ask yourself *why* you want each particular thing. Dig deep, if you have to, for the answers. This is such an important question to ask and answer, because it provides even more clarity and detail to your initial desire. Understanding your "why" is crucial to removing blocks, and to getting clear on what we want.

⌘ Then complete the final column. How do you want to *feel* once you have this new desire in your life? Really feel those emotions, for they will help you raise your vibration around these new desires.

Checking in with our emotions is so important, because it helps maintain that balance of heart and head. The lists of what we don't and do want are often coming from our head, but the further exploration of *why* we want something and *how we feel* about it is coming from our heart.

If you feel resistance come up when you look at how you feel about your desires, this is where you can bring in the initial system of exploring and reprogramming your underlying beliefs.

⌘ What's the reason you're feeling resistance?
⌘ Where is it coming from? What's the underlying belief?
⌘ Is that underlying belief true?
⌘ Is it serving your higher good?
⌘ Does it need to be released and reprogrammed?
⌘ If so, what's the new, unlimited belief that you can fully embrace and live by?

Our reprogramming is a continuous process – we don't find all our hidden beliefs at once and then we're done. As we progress to getting clarity about what we want, we can find more underlying beliefs that have to be addressed so that we can move forward. So, don't be discouraged if these come up. Take comfort that you have found them, and that you have the reprogramming process to deal with them.

Address all of the reprogramming questions by closing your eyes, breathing deeply, and asking your Divine Self for the answers. They are all in there, I assure you. And, until you listen to those answers and start acting on them, you will remain stuck.

Complete this process for each of the ten areas of your life. The purpose of this exercise is to start getting really clear about what you want, and why you want it, so that you can set your intentions about creating what you desire.

Now, up to this point, we've been very focused on our inner work, but I want to take a moment to explain a fundamental principle behind your personal-transformation journey, or anything else that's happening in your life. The changes you are making can't just be metaphysical. That is, they can't just happen in our inner worlds, in our hearts and minds. That piece is crucial – but it's not the whole picture.

If we really want change, there has to be a physical element to it, as well. We can't just think and feel; we also have to *do*. Without doing, we can think and feel all we want, but things may not happen. Some people study the Law of Attraction, and believe that if they just think about manifesting something, they'll get it. But the reality is that even if they are perfectly aligned with their desire, open to receiving it, and in a space of acceptance and allowing, chances are they won't get what they want if they do nothing about it.

We have to take action in our lives. We have to take action that is in alignment with what we want. What do I mean? Well, I'll give you an example from my own life. Recently, my husband and I wanted to buy a new home. We were explicit about wanting it to be in one of three small communities in our area – all of which are in high demand, and where the few houses that ever come on the market are snapped up quickly.

We created a detailed list of what we wanted in the house: the size, the number of bedrooms and bathrooms, even the layout. We were specific about the price, the type of garage, and the needs of our dog. The list was pretty long. As we put it together, we were drawing from what we knew we wanted – in our hearts and minds. But, we didn't just create the list, meditate on it, send it out to the universe, and hope that a house would come along.

We also took action. We identified the exact homes we were interested in for each community; we met with our realtors; and we gave them the list and the maps with our target homes highlighted. We talked to people in the community where we were renting – our top choice for buying. We told them we really wanted to be homeowners in the community, and we spread the word that if any homes came on the market, to let us know. We were taking action in very real ways – engaging with our neighbors, and seeking out professional assistance.

Within just a few weeks of doing all this, we had found two homes. The first was in our second preferred community. Ultimately, the price for this was too high, but it met all our other needs. When we released the idea of this home and let it go, three days later a home in our current community came to us by word of mouth. It was the right price, the right layout, the right everything for us. It even had a built-in doggy door from the bedroom to the backyard, so we knew the house was perfect for all three of us. We had set our intentions, and created our reality, both metaphysically and physically.

That's just one example, but it's true for all areas of our lives: whether we're focused on relationships, work, money, health, community, spirituality, or whatever – we have to do the inner work, and we also have to take outward action in alignment with that.

We need both: the metaphysical and the physical. My personal preference is to start with the metaphysical because it makes the physical much easier. When we have clarity about what we want, why we want it, and how we want to feel when we get it, it provides a much clearer roadmap for what we need to do in the physical realm.

If we don't do our inner work first, we may end up spinning our wheels with a lot of doing – but seeing little to no results, because the end goal is so murky and undefined. So, getting clear is the first real step in creating what we want.

Once we have identified what we want, we need to get more precise. As I discovered, it's not enough to just have a goal and go for it. There needs to be more detail and definition to each goal or thing that we want to manifest. I've experienced this both ways in my professional life.

Take, for example, the experience I had when I got very clear about what I wanted, and was very specific in the details and the desires. This happened for me with my second job after college.

I was finishing up my MBA (Masters of Business Administration), and although I had settled on market research as my specialty, I really didn't know what I wanted to do with it. I had about six months left in the program, and I was unsure what would come next, but I knew I needed a paycheck to make my rent.

I started thinking about things I was interested in, and how I could match my skills, knowledge, and MBA to that. It came to me out of the blue while I was sitting on the couch one day. I was manipulating spreadsheets for my professor as part of my graduate-assistant work. It was tedious and boring, so I had turned on cable news to play in the background. At the time, I was a cable news junkie – I watched all the time, and I was always up to speed on every current event.

It suddenly dawned on me that cable news channels must do some kind of research for their brand and their competition. A light bulb went off. I could do research for a cable news channel! I was so thrilled with the breakthrough. I could match my skills with something I enjoy – what could be better? It was genius! Until those voices in my head started: "You don't know the first thing about the cable news business, you definitely don't have any experience, and there are only a handful of channels you could work for – how the heck are you gonna do that? This is a ridiculous idea!"

I was undeterred. I told everyone my plan: to get an unpaid internship at a cable news channel. Then I would either turn that into a full-time paid position, or use the experience to go to another channel and get a job. So, I set my intention in my heart and in my head, and I told the world – sending it out to the universe. It all seemed so logistically impossible. I was already dead broke, so taking an unpaid internship was nuts; I was in grad school and in my mid-twenties, whereas most interns are undergrads, age nineteen or twenty – and the channels were all in New York and North Jersey, whereas I lived in Philadelphia.

It didn't matter. I was clear about what I wanted, and I was determined. I got interviews with two channels, and I was offered both positions. I took the one that was more aligned with what I wanted to do: brand and market research. I was thrilled, even though I was working five days a week for nothing, and driving 200 miles each day to do it! Then, in my first few days on the job, I realized it was the wrong fit. I was in the wrong department. But I was so clear on what I wanted to do that I went to my supervisor with a defined project. She agreed: it wouldn't happen with me in *that* department, but she saw the value in it, and knew exactly where it *would* fit.

She introduced me to the vice-president of the department I would ultimately work for. I was scared. Up to this point I had been working for a small business that felt like a family. I'd never met a vice-president of a huge corporation one-on-one before! I had voices screaming at me from inside: "You're not good enough; you don't fit; you aren't smart enough for this; who do you think you are to be in this place based on where you came from?" It was all I could do to breathe, and not have sweaty palms when I shook her hand.

But again, because I singularly wanted to navigate this path, I presented my idea and waited for the response. She was intrigued, and wanted to do it. I couldn't believe it! After that, it was just a matter of moving across the large, open office to her department, and working with her team. I labored over that project as though my life depended on it. I worked late when I didn't have school, and I came in as early as I could, after my ninety-minute morning commute.

Before the end of my internship was even in sight, the vice-president was offering me a full-time position, and we were negotiating my title and compensation. I had truly manifested my dream. It was because I was so exceptionally clear on what I wanted, why I wanted it, how I wanted to feel – _and_ I took action. I did both my inner and outer work, and I had been very particular about what I wanted. Looking back, it's still amazing to me that I did it all. At the time there were only four cable news channels, each with a single position for what I wanted to do. I landed one of them, despite having no experience just six months earlier.

Now, take the example of where I wasn't so explicit or precise about my next goal, which was to make lots of money. It was clear in one respect: I wanted to prosper financially. But, that's where it ended. I had no clue how I wanted to make the money, nor how I could, or even how much I wanted to make. There were no real details attached to this ambition; it was more of a broad, general desire than a specific goal.

Still, I got what I wanted, because I was clear about the overall achievement. But without the details, the universe and my underlying beliefs essentially filled in the gaps, and I created by default a world I would ultimately give up – because it was not in alignment with me and what I was to be doing.

After a couple of years at the cable news channel, I'd morphed from being a general news junkie to being a political news junkie. I'd become fascinated by politics and policy, prompted by the events of September 11, 2001. So much was clear to me that day, and in the aftermath of what occurred, that I felt a strong desire to somehow become involved in the policy and direction of the country.

But, here I was again with no contacts, formal knowledge, or experience in the field. I knew I didn't want to go and work on a campaign, or join the national political committees. To me, that would be starting over at square one and taking a pay cut, which I was unwilling to do with an MBA and a few years in corporate America under my belt. So, I looked again at how I could I match the skills and knowledge I had with what I wanted to do. The answer: political or public-policy research.

I set my intention mentally and emotionally, then took action. I downloaded a list of every research firm in the Washington, D.C. area, and began working through it alphabetically. I'd come home from work, get dinner, and start on the list, checking out the websites to see if the companies had openings and if they'd be a good fit. Finally, in the "P's," I hit on a company whose website spoke to the strong sense of competition that I had back then. They only had one job opening, which I knew would be below where I wanted to start, but I sent my resume anyway. I got a call the next day, interviewed in D.C. three days later, and three weeks after that I was starting with the company in a position I wanted.

It was only after I started there that I realized I had no clue how to do the actual job, and that my learning curve would be incredibly steep. Looking back, it's clear that the people who hired me recognized this, but at the time I felt fraudulent and totally insecure that I had taken this job without the knowledge I needed to do it.

I went into an overdrive of commitment to get it done and be a success. I knew because of the way this company and its compensation system was structured that if I stayed there, I would make the "lots of money" I'd set out to do a few years earlier. But at what cost? It seems that I forgot that part – and I forgot to tune into my emotions.

I had a love-hate relationship with the company and the work from the very beginning. Sometimes, it was more hate than love, yet I stayed for eleven years, making partner after six. I broke every record there was to break – fastest promoted to every level, highest sales for first-year partner, and so on. But it ultimately meant nothing to me. I'd get a brief rush knowing that I had accomplished these things and seeing my bank account grow. But inside, I was dying a little more each day.

Although I started out by creating what I wanted in finding and getting this job, staying there for years was in fact denying myself love and joy in life. When I look back on that time now, I am overwhelmed with gratitude for all that I learned from the incredibly smart people I worked with. But it's as though I navigated that decade of my life on autopilot.

I missed so many of the signals that my body sent me – both emotionally and physically. I just stayed and stayed and stayed because I didn't see other options. I had said I wanted to make a lot of money, and I had done that. But what now? I was stuck.

The irony of this story is that only a couple of years before I took the job, the events of September 11, 2001 had greatly impacted me and brought a lot of clarity to my life. I am an immigrant. I was born and raised in Belfast, Northern Ireland. I went to Scotland for my undergraduate degree and moved to the United States right after graduation, getting my green card through employment sponsorship. I had been toying with the idea of becoming a citizen, but I was still unsure about it. September 11, 2001 changed that.

I drove home from work that night on the New Jersey Turnpike, watching the smoke billowing out of the Twin Towers and seeing a never-ending convoy of rescue vehicles headed toward New York from New Jersey, Pennsylvania, Delaware and Maryland. I was rocked to my core, as so many were that day. When I got home, I told my roommates, "I am an American. I am bleeding inside like the rest of you right now." After that day, there was no question in my mind. I would become a citizen as soon as my five-year green card waiting period was up.

The other big decision I made shortly after that was to get a tattoo. I had wanted one for a long time, but I could never answer the question of what I would want now, in my mid-twenties, that I'd still want on sagging skin at age seventy. But, clarity was there – I had the tattoo artist design an American flag with "Courage" written above it and "Freedom" written below it. He and everyone else who saw it asked me, "Huh? Why 'Courage' and 'Freedom'?" My response was clear and consistent: "Because if you have courage and freedom in your life, you have everything you'll ever need. Everything else happens as a byproduct of having those two elements in your life."

What a profound thought – way back in 2001. Here I was, walking around with my roadmap for life inked on my body, and I totally forgot it was there. If only I'd looked at my tattoo more often! I already had two of the highest-vibrating emotions staring at me in the mirror:

courage and freedom. I already knew the answers, but I had closed myself off to this part of me and fallen asleep to what was possible.

It wasn't until twelve years later, when I started doing all my inner work and going through my personal-transformation process, that I realized I'd had the answers all along – if I have courage and freedom, then I can be who I really am and do whatever I choose.

I tell this story for two reasons. First, to make the point that sometimes what we need to know is staring us right in the face, and we already know it. Second, as a reminder that even if you feel stuck now, there was probably a time in your life when you didn't feel so stuck, and things were much clearer and easier to define.

As we do our reprogramming and use the other processes I've laid out in this book, we can return to that clarity. We can start to really move forward, with courage and freedom, to desire and create the life we really want.

For me, it was those early days when I didn't have money and I was just starting out in my career. I was singularly focused on getting to a place where I could prosper financially. I ultimately did that, but I put the rest of myself to sleep in the process. I learned that being clear on one aspect of your life, and shutting down the rest, doesn't leave much room for anything else.

It's important to be clear about what we want in all aspects of our life because they are all connected – and to check in constantly with our emotions to make sure we're still on the path that's right for us, and that we haven't veered off course on autopilot.

Chapter 12
Finding Your Calling and Higher Purpose

When we get clarity about what we want, and we take action to create and manifest that in our lives, we are getting ourselves unstuck. As we move into this new phase in our life, we can also move toward what we're really here for – our higher purpose, our calling.

When we start raising our vibration, it can often mean stepping outside of what we're comfortable and secure with. It may mean moving into unknown or uncharted territory – and that can be frightening to so many of us. Even though the idea of leaving my long-held position in research was extraordinarily appealing to me, and I felt joy and hopefulness when I thought about this, I was also terrified of what lay beyond.

I didn't know what I would do. I had spent so long in that role that it was tough for me to imagine doing anything different. In fact, I often felt that leaving it behind would be like falling off a cliff into an abyss of darkness. Yet, something within me kept whispering that it wouldn't be darkness; it would be light – light beyond my wildest imagination. The truth was that I had already been living in darkness for so long, that staying there felt more comfortable.

Raising our vibration helps us move from dark to light. We start to see things with much more clarity. I understood this at some deep, core level, and it's why I finally made the decision to leave. But, that decision was not the final resting point. Far from it. It was just the beginning.

Moving into the light, where everything is visible, would mean really stepping into who I am – and that was still a work in progress. I vacillated back and forth for about a year on my decision to leave. One day, the frustration of the work would be too much, and it would propel me toward leaving. The next day, it wouldn't seem that bad, and I could just keep going with what I was used to.

What really made me see that I had to leave it behind was not the pain of the situation – although that certainly provided contrast to help me get clarity on what I did want. It was the realization that in reprogramming my beliefs, and now truly believing in myself and what I was capable of, I understood that staying where I was meant not following my dreams – and not discovering my calling.

I didn't know yet what my calling was, so it was challenging for me to articulate this to anyone other than my husband and my coaches, but I just knew there was *more* that I was to be doing with my life.

What is a higher purpose or calling? It is knowing that there is something greater to your life that you're meant to be doing. Often it means helping others, or giving of yourself, your time, or your resources, in a way that can contribute to making the world a better place. This can be any manner of things. It might be playing beautiful music, creating inspiring artwork, working at a food kitchen for the homeless, donating to charity, mentoring young people, running a softball team at work, coaching your son's Little League team. It doesn't have to be what you do for a living, although some people are blessed to fulfill their calling and derive income from it.

There are so many ways that we can have a greater calling, where we're asked to step out of our regular lives and do something that is beyond our comfort zone. Those who have done this will tell you about the fears associated with the process, but they will also be very quick to tell you that it's worth every nerve-wracking moment, because it has brought them so much meaning, joy, and fulfillment.

I discovered that my calling is to write, to coach, and to speak – to share with the world my experiences and what I have I learned – in the hope that it may help you, and others, navigate through struggles, and move to a place of freedom and joy in your life.

I am thankful to have my calling now also be my work. However, it took me a long time to understand that this was my higher purpose. It took me quite a while to clear the murkiness of my old beliefs and stop listening to all those negative tracks, before I could open my heart and start trusting my Divine Self and my intuition.

As I worked through my journey of personal transformation and got really clear about what I wanted in all aspects of my life, I started noticing opportunities and ideas opening up to me. It was truly my Divine Self and my intuition that brought me to life coaching. I received a signal and followed it, despite my ego throwing up multiple reasons not to. Just after I had resigned from the company I'd been with for eleven years, I stumbled upon the idea – even though, once again, it had been staring me in the face for quite some time.

I received an email from a source whose material I usually delete without reading, since it rarely resonates with me. But, on this particular day, I felt compelled to open it and see what it had to say. It was announcing a life-coaching certification course, and to watch five days' worth of videos to learn more.

Of course, my ego immediately kicked in and said, "I don't have time to watch a video every day for the next five days. If they can't tell me what I need to know in this email, then this is not for me." But something was drawing me forward: bringing me to a new place, a new sense of possibility. I diligently watched the videos. In fact, one of them didn't get delivered on the expected day, so I emailed the organization and chased it down. I was clearly intrigued and hooked by what this program had to offer. But a big part of me was scared and uncertain.

My ego tried to throw me off in many ways. It wanted real, hard facts and evidence to justify the decision. I knew I wanted to do it, but I heard myself saying to my husband and others, "Well, it wasn't that expensive. It's a full certification, but it's flexible in that I do it part time for a year, online and over the phone. So, there's not much to lose. Even if I don't ultimately want to become a life coach, at least I'll have learned a lot. I'll have the experience, and it won't have cost me much financially." Gee, what a ringing endorsement that was. Could I have hedged my bets any better? I was listening to and answering my ego. Even with all those justifications, it still felt uncomfortable moving forward, but something deep within me propelled me to sign up. My Divine Self and my heart were quietly excited and fascinated by this new adventure.

As my former professional life drifted away, I was able to dedicate more time to the life-coaching course. I found new space and clarity to read, study, and practice. To my ego's surprise, I liked it! I really liked it! I enjoyed helping people get relief, and seeing their breakthrough "aha" moments. I had an epiphany: All I've ever wanted to do is help people and see them be happy. This is the perfect fit for me. My heart was singing a happy tune, but I was still being scared and silenced by my ego and its negative chatter.

I struggled internally with the shift I was making. I would describe it as moving from the "linear and tangible" (research/data/head-driven) to the "soft and fluffy" (feelings/intuition/heart-driven). It was as though I was doing a 180-degree turn with my skill set and knowledge – and it was certainly taking me way beyond my comfort level. I wasn't yet confident in talking about feelings, or in gauging others' emotions or energetic vibrations.

Even though I had been seeing a life coach for a year at this point myself, in many ways this world still felt new to me. Most of the language and concepts of personal development were very different from what I had been living for so long. It was one thing to be coached and to understand various different concepts; it was another thing to be able to effectively articulate these ideas and coach others.

It was a whole new realm for me. The negative voices kept chattering, but I just kept putting them aside and following my heart, for I was loving every minute of this new personal-development world. It truly resonated with me. I was reading every book I could get my hands on, attending workshops, and immersing myself deeply in the process. I knew that I was being drawn to this way of life, this way of thinking, this new way of perceiving and looking at things. And, it felt good. It felt *really* good!

Yet, at the same time, I was compelled to hide it from the world. My ego had me so worried about what others would think of my going in this direction. I'd play in my mind what I thought people would say. "What's up with this fluffy life coaching? Have you lost your mind? Where did logical and research-minded Alex go?" I was allowing my ego to run amuck with its negative tracks.

The reality was far different, and now I understand why. When we step into what we're called to do, we are taken very seriously. People can sense the vibration of energy from us; they understand that this is no joke. They can also perceive qualities and aspects of us that we don't always see ourselves – probably because we're too busy listening to our negative chatter.

The few people I felt comfortable sharing my new path with were immediately encouraging and supportive. In fact, none of them were surprised, and they saw it as a natural progression for me. They saw nothing "fluffy" about it. I realized the perception of fluffy had nothing to do with others at all. I was simply projecting my own fears and concerns onto them. My former employer at the cable news channel, and now a former client, proclaimed, "This is perfect for you!"

She explained that I had just spent the last fifteen years coaching corporations, organizations, and people within them on their projects, brands, and competition – so coaching individuals about their lives was an obvious next step. As she said that, a light bulb went off in my head. I had been worried about who I was going to help; what my platform and message should be. And it was right in front of me all along – kind of like that tattoo I needed to pay more attention to.

The people I am called to help are dealing with some of the struggles I have experienced. They want something more from life; they know life can be better; but they may not know exactly how to get there. I know these feelings, these worries, and these desires, because I have lived them. I have lived with angst, insecurity, struggle, frustration, and an overall sense of being stuck. That's when I realized my calling was to unstick people. To help them move to a new place, to realize their true potential – and to find their true meaning in life.

Upon unearthing this revelation, I was further motivated to build my coaching practice, to write this book, and to move my life to a whole new level where I am now serving many people. My hope is that in doing so, I am also helping the world by bringing more and more people into their conscious awakening, raising their energy vibration, and reconnecting with their Divine Selves.

Identifying Your Calling or Higher Purpose

Recurring Themes/Desires For What I Want	The Skills I Have Learned	My Natural Talents

You see, just as I had a roadmap tattooed on my body that I could have been following all along, we all have a blueprint of divine guidance within us. We just need to access it, and to reach for those feelings that take us to a new level.

It's Your Turn:

Here are some specific steps that *you* can take to help you connect the dots, and tap into what might be *your* calling or higher purpose.

- ⌘ Take the ten pages you created in the previous chapter and look at the right-hand side of each one, at all the lists of what you want and why you want those things.
- ⌘ As you look through these lists, are there recurring themes? Are there desires for specific feelings, or items that show up in multiple areas of your life? What are they? Take a new piece of paper and jot them down in a list.
- ⌘ Next to these recurring themes and concepts, create two more columns and label them "Skills" and "Talents" as shown on the opposite page. The difference between these is that skills are learned, while talents are naturally present. For example, you may be skilled in specific computer software programs because you learned how to use them, while being neat and organized is a natural talent that you've had your whole life.

⌘ List all the skills and talents that you know you have. Don't hold back, and don't leave anything out. Include all the skills and talents you can think of – big and small. Connect with your Divine Self as you do this, so that the ego chatter doesn't get in your way.

⌘ Now, look at the recurring themes of what you do want in the first column, and compare this with your skills and talents in the next two columns. Where are the overlapping areas? How could you achieve what you want with the skills and talents you already have? How could you try out or experiment with these new ideas or new possibilities? Is there some additional training or learning you may need, to help build the bridge from where you are to where you want to be?

_____

_____

_____

_____

_____

You may not get the answers immediately, but this exercise will help to stimulate creativity deep within. It also begins to uncover the holistic nature of our lives. We've been taking individual life categories and identifying what we want, why we want it, and how we want to feel. But, as we look over all these lists, we find recurring themes: concepts and desires that emerge in all aspects of our lives, because they are all connected. These recurring ideas or desires are the crux of what we want. When we understand that fundamental core, then we can start looking at what physical form it might take in our lives – whether it's volunteering, a career, or a hobby that we love.

As I look back at the "aha" moment on discovering my calling, I can see clearly now that the recurring theme for what I wanted in many areas of my life was to help people and to be of service. I realized that so many of the skills I learned in my research career had perfectly prepared me for my new career in coaching, writing, and speaking. This wasn't the 180-degree turn I had thought of at the time. I had already been doing all of these things, just on a different platform. I also realized that one of my natural talents is to connect and communicate with people at all levels, and in all walks of life. I had been doing that my whole life, and now I could use it for a higher purpose: to help people get unstuck, find their way, and be happy.

The rewards are huge. If you embrace your inner guidance, clear your mind, and work these processes, you can be and do anything you want. Even better, if you align you heart, your head, and your metaphysical vibration with physical action you can create the life you want, fulfill the dreams you've always wanted, and find your calling or higher purpose.

Marianne Williamson, the wonderful spiritual guide and teacher, has a beautiful quotation that I read to myself often as a reminder of the unlimited power inside all of us, and what we can do with it:

> *"Our deepest fear is not that we are inadequate. Our deepest fear is that we are powerful beyond measure. It is our light, not our darkness that most frightens us. We ask ourselves, 'Who am I to be brilliant, gorgeous, talented, fabulous?' Actually, who are you not to be? You are a child of God. Your playing small does not serve the world. There is nothing enlightened about shrinking so that other people won't feel insecure around you. We are all meant to shine, as children do. We were born to make manifest the glory of God that is within us. It's not just in some of us; it's in everyone. And as we let our own light shine, we unconsciously give other people permission to do the same. As we are liberated from our own fear, our presence automatically liberates others."*

I love this passage because it reminds me of the vastness inside all of us, and that we each have a calling for a higher purpose, and a divine right to shine brightly in this lifetime.

Now, it's up to you. It's your turn. Are you going to play it small, stay in your lane, and stay stuck? Or, are you going to embrace where you are right now, get clear, release the old negative beliefs and lower-vibrating feelings, forgive the past, believe in yourself, and move toward the light?

When we move into the light, we can get clear on who we really are, and what it is that we're meant to be doing – our higher purpose, our calling. We can start to come from a place of love, abundance, and creativity; instead of lack, fear, and being stuck.

When we come from lack and fear, we are often setting the tone for what is to be. We're sending out that low-level vibration, so we're going to get more of that back. If we think that nothing works for us, then nothing ever will. Instead, if we come from a place of abundance and love, we are sending out a higher-level vibration, and that's what we'll get back. We'll create and manifest what we want.

So, let's review your roadmap to the life you want to create:

We need both inner and outer work to achieve balance.

Begin with the inner work so that the outer work will be easier.

Reprogram: Start by looking at situations in your life that cause you distress, or that bother you. Begin with an area you know you want to change, rather than one where you may be resistant to change.

- ⌘ Examine how you feel when these situations occur, and how you feel after they happen.
- ⌘ Just breathe into those feelings, acknowledge them, and accept them for what they are – because they can't hurt you now.

⌘ Ask yourself why you feel that way. What's the underlying belief or thought that's driving the feeling?

⌘ Where did that underlying belief come from? Can you accept that it's been there for a long time?

⌘ Ask yourself if that underlying belief is your truth, and if it is in alignment with your higher good.

⌘ If it's not, are you ready to release it, and embrace a new belief that will be part of your new program?

⌘ Create a new, positive belief that feels good, that you can embrace and live as you move forward.

⌘ Get in front of a mirror: look deep into your eyes, and say that belief to yourself.

⌘ Use this new belief as your affirmation, and practice saying it both inwardly and out loud each day.

⌘ If any resistance comes up, sit with it; then ask where is it coming from, and is it true? Is there a different truth you are to believe in?

⌘ Work through the resistance as you work through your underlying beliefs. Accept the thoughts and feelings that come up, but question if they are really your truth.

⌘ Connect and communicate with your Divine Self to give yourself the love, respect, and support you deserve every day.

You can use this process for any situation or issue that presents itself in your life. If you want to identify the root cause, and change things as you move forward, this is the work that sets the foundation.

Raise Your Vibration: As you build the foundation of reprogramming your deeply held beliefs, you can also develop the next step of raising your vibration: releasing the negative, being in a place of acceptance and allowing, practicing gratitude, and being open to receive, while consciously choosing your thoughts and feelings.

⌘ Get into the habit of "no judgment": accept people and situations for who and what they are. This doesn't mean you have to like or condone something, just that you accept it.

⌘ Instead of looking for the bad, look for the good. When you find yourself about to criticize or complain, pause for a moment and see if you can find the goodness, the higher quality of the person or situation.

⌘ Practice gratitude. Get a journal, and every day, write down three to five things for which you are grateful. Give thanks for all the goodness and wondrous gifts you have all around you and within you. Find different things each day to be thankful for.

⌘ Be aware of your energy and your emotions. Look for ways to reach for higher vibrations, and better-feeling thoughts and perceptions.

As you reprogram your underlying beliefs, release the negative ones and the judgment, and move into a place of acceptance and gratitude, you will notice the shift within yourself as your vibration rises. You will feel more open, more alive, than ever before. You will be awakened and free. That stuckness you have lived with for so long will lift, and you will move from darkness and contraction into light and expansion.

Use the Everyday Tools: Brighten that light by using the techniques that can clear space for your heart and mind.

- ⌘ Meditate daily.
- ⌘ Take on the role of observer.
- ⌘ Set boundaries and learn to say no.
- ⌘ Separate the needs from the wants.

Explore and Expand the Possibilities: Get clear on what you really want, and start to explore your calling or higher purpose.

- ⌘ Start by identifying – in every aspect of your life – the things you do not want, how these things make you feel, and the reason you no longer want them.
- ⌘ Based on what you *don't* want, in every aspect of your life, identify what you really *do* want.
- ⌘ Look at *why* you want those things, and how you want to *feel* when you have them.

⌘ Look for patterns or recurring themes around what you want, and identify the fundamental core of your desires.

⌘ Compare the recurring themes to the lists of talents and skills you already have, and see where there is overlap or potential for new possibilities.

⌘ Set your intentions internally, and consult with your Divine Self to confirm that you are on the right path.

⌘ Take action that is aligned with your intentions. Do something each day that moves you closer to your dreams and desires.

Take the challenge, try these things, and see how your life changes. If I can do it, anyone can. It took me many years to figure it all out. It doesn't have to take that long, or be that difficult, for you. Use the tools I have provided in this book, and realize your potential to create the life you truly want to live. Right here. Right now.

About the Author

A lex Bratty is an author and life coach. Her work helps people transform their lives by empowering them with personal development techniques, resources, and processes so they can take action to create and live the life they truly want.

After a fifteen-year career in research, five of which she spent as a partner in a prestigious Washington, D.C. firm, Alex knew something was missing; that she wasn't fulfilling her life's purpose.

In her quest to find that missing piece, Alex embarked on a personal-development journey that opened her mind and soul to the realization that she could be both personally happy and professionally fulfilled. Until then, these elements had been almost mutually exclusive and compartmentalized in her life. In combining them, she discovered that she could truly live the life she wanted.

Alex realized that the true essence of what she desired was to help people and to be of service in a way that would contribute positively to the world. She chose to write and to become a life coach to fulfill this calling. Alex understood that she had to share her experience of getting unstuck; of changing from a life that felt constricted, frustrated, and tense to one that was expansive, joyful, and relaxed.

Her deepest hope is that her book, and her coaching, will help others who are having similar experiences to embark on their own process of change and growth, to navigate their challenges more easily – and to help them get unstuck and create an amazing life that they love. She lives by the belief that we can all find happiness, abundance, and joy; that we just need to discover what we truly *do* want, rather than what we think we *should* want.

Alex earned her Bachelor's degree at Edinburgh University in Scotland, with dual honors in Business Studies and French in 1997. She then attained her Masters of Business Administration degree, from Villanova University in Pennsylvania, in 2001. After many years on the East Coast, she now lives in Las Vegas with her husband and their Golden Retriever, Sunny.

Connect with Alex and contact her at
alex@alexbratty.com

www.alexbratty.com
www.alexbrattybooks.com